IELTS express

Upper Intermediate

Coursebook

Richard Hallows

Martin Lisboa

Mark Unwin

with Pamela Humphreys

THOMSON

Australia • Canada • Mexico • Singapore • Spain • United Kingdom • United States

IELTS Express Upper Intermediate, **Coursebook**
Hallows / Lisboa / Unwin

Publisher: *Christopher Wenger*
Director of Product Development: *Anita Raducanu*
Director of Product Marketing: *Amy Mabley*
Editorial Manager: *Sean Bermingham*
Development Editor: *Derek Mackrell*
Production Editor: *Tan Jin Hock*
Editorial Assistant: *Esther de Rozario*
International Marketing Manager: *Ian Martin*
Sr. Print Buyer: *Mary Beth Hennebury*
Project Manager: *Howard Middle/HM ELT Services*
Production Management: *Process ELT*

Contributing Writers: *Mark Harrison and Russell Whitehead*
Contributing Development Editors: *G. Zographou, L. Darrand*
Copy Editor: *Lisa Darrand*
Compositor: *Process ELT*
Illustrator: *Bill Pandos*
Cover/Text Designer: *Studio Image & Photographic Art* (www.studio-image.com)
Printer: *G. Canale & C S.p.a*
Cover Image: *Michael Dunning/Getty Images*

Printed in Italy.
1 2 3 4 5 6 7 8 9 10   10 09 08 07 06

For more information contact Thomson Learning, High Holborn House, 50/51 Bedford Row, London WC1R 4LR United Kingdom or Thomson ELT, 25 Thomson Place, Boston, Massachusetts 02210 USA. You can visit our web site at elt.thomson.com

ISBN: 1-4130-0963-8

Text Credits
Page 9: From "The Getaway Blues" by Patrick Sawer. Copyright © The Evening Standard (28 April 2004). Pages 21 and 22: From Times Higher Education Supplement/Higher Education Statistics Agency. Page 23: From Times Higher Education Supplement/British Council. Page 23: From www.ielts.com. Page 26: From www.Open2.net. Copyright © 2005 The Open University. Page 54: From "Environmental Enemy No. 1." Copyright © The Economist Newspaper Limited, London (4 July 2002). Page 74: From "Look Who Was Talking" by Stephen Oppenheimer © Stephen Oppenheimer 2003. Page 70: From "Space Odyssey" by Jonathan Glancey. Copyright © Guardian Newspapers Limited 2003. Page 94: From "If It Whines It Must Be Gold," by Elizabeth Grice. Copyright © Telegraph Group Limited 2003. Page 98: From "Only the Eagle-eyed Will Spot a Fake," by David Attenborough. Copyright © Telegraph Group Limited 2004. Page 101: From "For Imaginary Ailments, Some Real Treatments," by Mary Duenwald. Copyright © 2004 by the New York Times Co. Page 103: Copyright © New York Times.

Photo Credits
Pages 8 & 13 © IT Stock Free; page 16, left & right © BananaStock; page 20 © Stockdisc; page 30, courtesy of Philips Electronics; pages 31 & 38 © Comstock Images; page 42 © BananaStock; page 52 © Corbis Images; page 57 © Stockbyte; page 60 © ImageState; page 64, centre © Stockbyte; page 64, right © Corbis Images; page 70 © John Keogh; page 77 © Associated Press/Frank Franklin II; page 82, top left © Oxford Scientific; page 82, top middle © Blend Images; page 82, top right © Goodshoot; page 89, left © BananaStock; page 89, right © Stockbyte. All other photos from Photos.com.

Additional artwork on page 47 by Bill Pandos, based on art on page 52 of "Grow Your Own Vegetables" by Joy Larkcom, publisher: Frances Lincoln (4 Torriano Mews, Torriano Ave., London NW5 2RZ), 2002.

Author Acknowledgements
The authors would like to jointly thank the editors, Sean Bermingham, Derek Mackrell, Lisa Darrand and Georgia Zographou for their considerable creative input, hard work and dedication to this project; Pamela Humphreys for her invaluable contributions; Howard Middle, project consultant, for his superb problem solving skills; and Chris Wenger the publisher for his good humour and showing us all a good time. We would also like to thank Loukas Ioannou's team for such a great job with the design.

Martin:
A big thank you to colleagues and students at the English Language Centre, London Metropolitan University for trialling material and offering sound advice and support. Thanks to my Dad for unravelling the mysteries of how LCD TVs function for Unit 3. Finally, to my wife Manuela and my son Max, a very special thank you for tolerating me spending far too much time in front of the computer screen – without your support, good humour and inspiration, this book would have been impossible.

Richard:
I'd like to thank Matt for being really supportive and for listening to me going on and on.

Mark:
Rubbage to Queenie, Bumble and – especially – SJC.

What is IELTS?

IELTS (International English Language Testing System) is a globally recognised English language exam, designed to assess the language ability of candidates who need to study or work where English is the language of communication. It is accepted by the majority of universities and further education colleges in the UK, Australia, Ireland, New Zealand, Canada, South Africa as well as a large number of institutions in the United States. It is also recognised by professional bodies, immigration authorities and other government agencies. IELTS is jointly managed by the University of Cambridge ESOL Examinations (Cambridge ESOL), the British Council and IDP: IELTS Australia.

IELTS is offered in two formats – Academic and General Training. All candidates take the same Listening and Speaking modules and there is an option of either Academic or General Training Reading and Writing modules. Academic is suitable for students wishing to enter an undergraduate or postgraduate study programme. General Training is suitable for candidates planning to undertake non-academic training, or work experience, or for immigration purposes. Further information about the exam can be obtained from the IELTS website www.ielts.org.

What is the *IELTS Express* series?

IELTS Express is a two-level exam preparation course at Intermediate level (IELTS Band 4–5.5) and Upper Intermediate level (IELTS Band 5 and above). *IELTS Express Intermediate* covers both Academic and General Training test formats; *IELTS Express Upper Intermediate* is designed for candidates aiming for higher scores in the Academic exam. Both levels of the *IELTS Express* series focus on building skills and providing essential exam practice. In addition to the Coursebook, each level of *IELTS Express* comprises the following components:

Workbook
The Workbook contains vocabulary and grammar tasks, skills building tasks and exam practice tasks. It is suitable for classroom or self-study use, and is accompanied by a separate audio component for additional speaking and listening practice.

Teacher's Guide
The Teacher's Guide provides detailed guidance on how to approach the Coursebook tasks and suggestions about extending these tasks. In addition, there are notes on how to adapt the material according to the level of your students. Practice test answers and model essays for the writing tasks are also included. The Teacher's notes are designed for both experienced teachers of IELTS and teachers who are unfamiliar with the exam.

Video/DVD
The Video/DVD shows students taking a simulated IELTS Speaking exam with an IELTS examiner. It includes commentary from the examiner on the candidates' performance, with particular reference to the skills practised in the Speaking sections of the Coursebook.

Audio Tapes/CDs
The Audio Tapes/CDs contain all the recorded material from the Coursebook, including listening tasks and model answers for all the Speaking sections.

IELTS Express is designed to work flexibly for courses of any length. For short courses, the Coursebook can be used to provide approximately 30–40 hours teaching time. For longer courses, *IELTS Express Intermediate* and *IELTS Express Upper Intermediate Coursebooks* can be taught consecutively, providing approximately 60–80 hours teaching time. This can be further extended if combined with *IELTS Express Workbooks* and videos/DVDs.

IELTS Express Upper Intermediate

How is the book organised?

The book is divided into eight theme-based units covering a broad range of typical IELTS topic areas. Each unit covers one productive skill and one receptive skill. Units 1, 3, 5 and 7 consist of a Reading and Speaking section, while Units 2, 4, 6, and 8 consist of a Listening and Writing section.

IELTS Express Upper Intermediate Coursebook also includes:

- three **Progress tests** that review and practise the exam tasks presented in previous units
- a complete **Practice test** for the Academic module
- a **Writing bank** with annotated model answers for the writing tasks
- an **Answer key** for all unit exercises
- **Listening scripts** for all the recorded material
- a **Language bank** of useful expressions for the speaking and writing exam tasks

How is each unit section organised?

Each unit section (Reading, Speaking, Listening and Writing) consists of the following:

- an **Introduction** which presents the topic through discussion questions and/or a task on key vocabulary
- **skills development** tasks
- **exam practice** tasks
- an **In the exam** box which gives detailed information on a particular part or section of the exam
- **For this task** boxes which offer step-by-step guidance and general strategies for tackling each task
- **Express tips** which highlight points to remember when taking the exam

Each writing section includes a **model essay** and each speaking section includes an **audio recording** of a model answer.

After every two units is a **Progress test**. These tests contain realistic IELTS questions that reflect the task types and exam sections covered in the previous units, as well as providing students with additional practice of essential skills. Students can use these tests to check their progress and to identify any areas of difficulty that need reviewing. Following Unit 8 is a full-length IELTS **Practice test** that completes the course.

The Progress tests and Practice test can be set under exam conditions in class or attempted individually during private study. Detailed answers for all the tests, including explanations and annotated listening scripts, are included in the *IELTS Express Upper Intermediate Teacher's Guide*.

Acknowledgements

The authors and publishers would like to thank all those who participated in the development of the project:

Gill Atkinson, The British Council, Singapore

Elizabeth Au, The British Council, Kuala Lumpur, Malaysia

Lucas Bak, The British Council, Seoul, Korea

Julia Boardwell, PLAN, Nagoya, Japan

Crispin Davies, EF, Cambridge, England

Belinda Hardisty, Studio Cambridge, Cambridge, England

Lee Hewson, The British Council, Hanoi, Vietnam

Kirsten Holt, St. Giles International, Eastbourne, England

Carmel Milroy, The British Council, Hanoi, Vietnam

Katherine Morris, The British Council, Naples, Italy

Karima Moyer, Universita' di Siena, Siena, Italy

Daniela Panayotova, EF, Cambridge, England

Guy Perring, The British Council, Tokyo, Japan

Vincent Smidowicz, Sidmouth International School, Sidmouth, England

Colin Thorpe, The British Council, Seoul, Korea

Emma Wheeler, The British Council, Hong Kong

Ying Xiong, Beijing New Oriental School, Beijing, China

In addition, the authors and publishers would like to express their gratitude to Mark Harrison and Russell Whitehead for their invaluable contribution to the series.

Leisure Activities

▸ **Exam tasks** ▸ Matching headings to paragraphs; summary completion; short-answer questions
▸ **Skills** ▸ Approaching the text; skimming for main ideas; scanning for keywords

1 Introduction

A Discuss these questions with a partner.

- When was the last time you went on holiday?
- What did you do on holiday?
- Was your holiday stressful or relaxing? Why?
- What would your perfect holiday be?

B Categorise the following into three groups. Label the words: calm (C), quite stressed (Q) or stressed (S).

a little frustrated	pretty anxious	somewhat nervous	slightly edgy
relaxed	really stressed out	incredibly uptight	utterly unstressed

C Think of situations or activities that make you feel some of the above emotions. Compare your ideas with a partner. Then ask questions to find out more about your partner.

2 Approaching the text

A Look at the title, subtitle, photo and first paragraph of the passage on the opposite page. Tell your partner what you think the text is about. Then skim the passage to decide the main theme. Were your predictions correct?

B Who do you think the article is aimed at? Where might you see this type of text? Discuss your ideas with a partner.

IN THE EXAM

Academic Reading module

The IELTS Reading module consists of three passages taken from books, magazines, journals or newspapers. The passages cover a variety of topics from scientific to historical interest, though the material will be targeted at a general, non-specialist audience.

The text will include titles and sometimes captions, photos and illustrations, which can help you to grasp the general meaning of the text. The total word length of all the texts can vary between 2,000 and 2,750 words.

There are forty questions in total, based on a variety of task types, such as matching headings to paragraphs, short-answer questions, multiple-choice and sentence completion.

The Reading module lasts one hour. No extra time is allocated at the end of the exam for transferring your answers onto the separate answer sheet, so it is recommended that you fill in your answers on the answer sheet as you complete each question. Pay careful attention to completing your answers in the correct order.

The getaway blues

Formula explains why it takes so long to relax on holiday

A With so much to do, going on holiday is certainly no vacation. First there's the flight to arrange, then the hotel or villa to book, and that's before you've sorted out the delicate matter of the beach outfit, evening wear and reading material.

B For much of the year we fantasise about a long break from the relentless drive of the everyday grind. But making our dream holiday a reality is what makes the stress really kick in, so it is little wonder it takes most holidaymakers a good few days to relax after their arrival. No matter how idyllic the surroundings, there's no immediate way to simply forget all about work, the children's schooling, the leaking roof and all those other domestic issues we long to escape.

C Susan Quilliam, psychologist, body language expert, and regular TV and radio commentator, states that stress creates actual changes in the body's hormonal balance and these take a while to dissipate. Ms Quilliam says that stress such as that caused by trying to arrange a holiday, creates hormonal changes in the body, including mood alteration. The result is that it takes the body a certain amount of time to regain its hormonal balance and become stress-free.

D We can suffer from anxiety, irritability and a range of more serious psychological problems including mild depression. The main point is that if we get stressed before the holiday, we may not be able to relax sufficiently to enjoy ourselves – often for several days after our arrival.

E Now we have a formula to calculate the amount of holiday time needed to recover from the stress of preparing for what should be our annual period of rest and recuperation. The formula, devised by Ms Quilliam,

---

Adding up the stress

$$\frac{P \times S}{H} = R$$

Key
P = Time spent preparing (hours)
S = Stress level of preparation (scale 0–9)
  0: utterly unstressed
  1: relaxed
  2: reasonably calm
  3: a little frustrated
  4: slightly edgy
  5: somewhat nervous
  6: pretty anxious
  7: really stressed out
  8: incredibly uptight
  9: stressed to the max
H = Stress level of the holiday
  If your holiday is a high-pressure tour, divide by 5; if medium stress, by 10; if laid back, by 15.
R = Time needed before you can relax enough to enjoy the holiday (hours)

---

is calculated thus: time spent preparing for the holiday, multiplied by the level of stress caused by the preparation (on a scale of 0 to 9), then divided by the stress level of the holiday (on a scale of 1 to 15). The result is the number of recovery hours needed before relaxation is possible.

F Ms Quilliam points out that taking a holiday is no longer a question of catching a bus to the nearest seaside resort with your bucket and spade. Today's pressurised lifestyles mean that going on holiday is a lot more stressful. We not only have to organise foreign travel and negotiate long, complex journeys, we also have to settle our home and work matters before we go.

G Add in potential tension with travel partners and the psychological pressures of high expectations, and by the time we arrive at our destination, we're stressed to the max! So according to Ms Quilliam, the secret to a stress-free holiday is planning and having realistic expectations. This means concluding any unfinished work in the office and ensuring the children are sufficiently entertained during the trip.

H The results of a survey commissioned by Lloyds TSB bank and carried out by Ms Quilliam, have confirmed her theories; today's holidaymakers really are stressed out. More than 83 per cent of people surveyed admitted to getting 'severely stressed' in the run-up to their holiday. More than a quarter of people admitted to needing the first few days of their holiday to recover. Some became so anxious they left without making essential arrangements and forgot things such as feeding the cat (11 per cent), taking out travel insurance (20 per cent), and cancelling the milk (12 per cent). Amazingly, a tiny minority of travellers (a little over 1 per cent) actually forgot to tell their bosses they were going on holiday!

Source: *London Evening Standard*

3 Skimming for main ideas

A Skim the passage a second time and focus on the highlighted sentences in paragraphs A–D. These are known as topic sentences as they contain the main idea or 'topic' for each paragraph. Underline the topic sentence in each of the remaining paragraphs E–H.

B A good topic sentence is a paragraph summary which gives the general meaning of the paragraph.

> **express tip**
> Skimming involves 'running your eyes over the text' quickly to get a general idea of the text. It isn't always necessary to understand everything, so try to avoid reading every word.

1 Select the sentences that best summarise the following four paragraphs.

Paragraph A
a There are a lot of things to arrange in order to go on holiday.
b Holidays can be fun.

Paragraph B
a With so many things to worry about, it's impossible to relax immediately on holiday.
b People dream about the perfect holiday.

Paragraph C
a Hormonal changes in the body cause stress.
b The stress of arranging a holiday creates hormonal changes in the body that cause moodiness.

Paragraph D
a If we get stressed on holiday, we might not be able to relax for several days.
b There is a link between stress before and during a holiday.

2 Write sentence summaries for paragraphs E–H in the passage.

C The topic sentence is generally supported by an explanation, examples or facts which support the main idea of the paragraph. The IELTS exam tests your ability to distinguish between the main ideas and supporting ideas.

Here are the supporting examples for the main idea of Paragraph B. Find the supporting ideas for the other paragraphs. Write them in your own words.

Paragraph B

Main idea
With so many things to worry about, it's impossible to relax immediately on holiday.
Supporting ideas
• The cause of stress comes from dreaming of having a perfect holiday.
• Examples of holiday-related stress: work problems, leaking roof, children's schooling.

D Using the formula in the passage, calculate how much time you would need before you could enjoy a holiday.

4 Scanning for keywords

When looking for specific information to answer questions, you need to scan the passage to locate relevant keywords. Don't expect to find an exact word match between the passage and the exam question – look for synonyms, too.

A Read the following gapped sentences, then scan the passage for synonyms or paraphrases for the keywords underlined.

1 All year, we <u>imagine</u> how wonderful it would be to have a .... from <u>our daily working lives</u>.

2 Ms Quilliam is not only a leading psychologist, she is also an <u>authority</u> on ....

3 Ms Quilliam's survey found that <u>over 25 per cent</u> of people use the beginning of their holiday to ....

B Now complete the sentences above by filling in the gaps with words from the passage.

C Read the following questions and underline the keywords which you would scan for in the passage.

1 As well as selecting a swimming costume and more formal clothes for dinner, what else do holiday makers need to choose?   ....

2 What three psychological symptoms are associated with stress?   ....

3 Who asked Ms Quilliam to carry out her research?   ....

Now scan the passage quickly for the relevant section and answer the questions using words from the passage.

5 Matching headings to paragraphs

for this task

▶ For this question type you are asked to find a suitable paragraph heading from a list to match to the appropriate paragraph in the text.

▶ Not all the headings will match the paragraphs in the text, so there are extra headings which you do not need to use.

▶ Skim the text to identify the topic sentence and the main idea of each paragraph. Take care not to confuse the main idea with the supporting ideas. Then write your own summary in the margin. This will help you locate information more quickly.

▶ There are two types of headings: headings that summarise the information of a paragraph and headings that pick out key information in the paragraph. Read through the list of headings and match any obvious headings to the paragraphs, making sure you cross off each heading as you do so.

▶ Delete any headings which are distractors. These might include supporting information such as a sentence which contains information from a paragraph that is not part of the main idea of the paragraph and therefore not the correct answer.

Questions 1–8

The reading passage has eight paragraphs A–H.

Choose the correct heading for each paragraph from the list of headings below.

*Write the correct numbers **i–x** next to the paragraphs.*

List of Headings	
i	Holiday stress statistics
ii	Stressful 'perfect holidays'
iii	Complex holiday preparations
iv	Holiday complaints
v	Good advice for happy holidays
vi	A mathematical model
vii	Times have changed
viii	How to relax after a holiday
ix	Delayed relaxation
x	Physical and psychological effects of stress

1 Paragraph A   .....
2 Paragraph B   .....
3 Paragraph C   .....
4 Paragraph D   .....
5 Paragraph E   .....
6 Paragraph F   .....
7 Paragraph G   .....
8 Paragraph H   .....

6 Summary completion

for this task

▶ There are two types of summary completion questions. In the first type you must complete the gaps with exact words from the passage; do not use synonyms. In the second type you must take words from a given list. These are often synonyms or paraphrases of keywords in the passage. Be careful of your spelling and check for a maximum word limit.

▶ Read the gapped summary carefully and decide if it is a summary of the whole passage or just one part. If the summary refers to one part only, quickly locate the part of the passage it refers to.

▶ Read the gapped sentence and select the best word(s) based on meaning and grammatical compatibility: which word class is required? Do you need a gerund or infinitive? etc.

Questions 9–13

*Complete the summary below. Choose **NO MORE THAN THREE WORDS** from the passage for each answer.*

A leading psychologist has **9** .... a simple mathematical equation to work out the number of hours required at the beginning of a holiday to get over the stress of all the preparation before departure. The problem is that taking a holiday these days is much more of a stressful experience than it was in the past as a result of our **10** .... However, stress levels can be decreased by having **11** .... of the holiday and making sure you complete **12** .... before leaving. This was illustrated in the survey results, which showed that some holidaymakers didn't even remember to **13** .... before setting out on holiday.

7 Short-answer questions

for this task

▶ Short-answer questions usually refer to a particular part of the passage, so try to locate the relevant section in the text quickly. Remember that the questions will always follow the same order as the text.

▶ Focus on the keywords in the question. These are usually synonyms or paraphrases of keywords in the passage. Look for these and they will help you locate the answer accurately.

▶ Answer the questions using words taken directly from the text as far as possible.

Questions 14–17

*Answer the questions below using **NO MORE THAN THREE WORDS** for each answer.*

14 What kind of change can we experience in our bodies due to stress? ....

15 What can we use to calculate how much holiday time we need to recover from stress? ....

16 What did people use to take on holiday with them to a seaside resort? ....

17 How do most holidaymakers feel just before going on holiday? ....

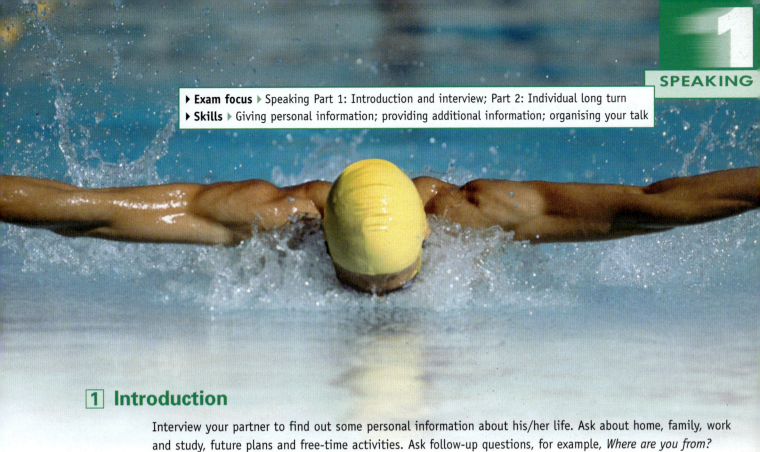

▶ **Exam focus** ▶ Speaking Part 1: Introduction and interview; Part 2: Individual long turn
▶ **Skills** ▶ Giving personal information; providing additional information; organising your talk

SPEAKING

1

1 Introduction

Interview your partner to find out some personal information about his/her life. Ask about home, family, work and study, future plans and free-time activities. Ask follow-up questions, for example, *Where are you from? How long have you been living there?*

2 Giving personal information

1.1 Listen to seven exam candidates answering some questions (1–7). You will hear the answers only. What question do you think the examiner asked each candidate? Write the questions down, then role-play the questions with a partner. Take it in turns to play the role of examiner and candidate.

3 Providing additional information

A **1.1** The candidates you heard in Exercise 2 extend their answer by giving additional information. What extra information do they give? Listen again and make notes.

1 One brother ...   .
2 I really enjoy speaking it ...   .
3 Not really ...   .
4 I work in McDonald's ...   .
5 I don't know exactly what I want to do ...   .
6 I'm from Sao Paolo in Brazil ...   .
7 I really enjoy science subjects ...   .

express tip

There is no right or wrong answer in this section. Extend your answer to make the listener interested in what you are saying.

B Ask and answer the questions in Exercise 2 again with a different partner. This time include additional information to give fuller answers.

IN THE EXAM

Speaking module: overview – Parts 1 and 2

The Speaking module consists of three parts. In all three parts, you will be evaluated on fluency and coherence, lexical resource, grammatical range and accuracy, and pronunciation. In Parts 1 and 2 you will use a variety of speech functions, including giving personal information, describing and explaining and expressing preferences.

This unit deals with Parts 1 and 2, which comprise personal questions relating to the candidate. You might be asked about your family, home, job, studies or other familiar topics. There are no right or wrong answers, but you will be expected to give full responses. This part of the module lasts about 4–5 minutes.

4 Introduction and interview

for this task

▶ Introduce yourself briefly.

▶ Listen to the examiner's questions carefully.

▶ Add extra information to extend your answers.

▶ Keep your answers relevant to the question.

▶ Use a variety of speech functions.

▶ Keep the marking criteria in mind.

▶ Speak fluently, connecting your ideas together logically.

▶ Make longer, more grammatically complex sentences.

▶ Use a wide range of vocabulary.

▶ Ensure you pronounce keywords correctly.

Work with a partner. In pairs, role-play Part 1 of the Speaking module.

Student A: You are the examiner. Choose some questions from Exercise 2. For each question, think of follow-up questions and interview Student B for four to five minutes. Listen to Student B's answers carefully. Do they extend their answers? What extra information is given?

Student B: You are the candidate. Imagine you are in the exam. Introduce yourself briefly, then listen to the questions and answer as fully as possible. Give extra information for each question.

When you have finished, change roles.

5 Organising your talk

A In Part 2 of the Speaking module, you are given a topic card asking you to describe an event or experience and then explain something connected with that event or experience.

Look at this topic card from Part 2 of the Speaking module.

> **Describe a sporting event that you have been to.**
> **You should say:**
> what it was
> why you went there
> what you saw exactly
> **and explain why you enjoyed or didn't enjoy it.**

In the exam you will be given one minute to prepare your talk. Here are a candidate's notes for the topic card above. With a partner, decide which points should be included in the answer. Put the relevant points in the correct order. Are any points irrelevant?

→ he won the breaststroke – very exciting – I felt proud

→ swimming – keep fit

→ went to see my boyfriend in swimming competition – charity event

→ I used to play tennis at school

→ lots of races – freestyle, breaststroke, backstroke, butterfly

→ I wanted to support him – first big competition

 B 1.2 Now listen to the candidate answering the question in the exam. Check your answers and listen for any extra information the candidate gives.

C Here is another candidate's notes for Part 2 of the Speaking module.

→ sports day at school
→ my race 400-metre relay race
→ fast runner – but didn't win
→ sat and watched – saw friends in races, long jump/high jump
→ Stephan – 2nd in the high jump
→ fun – relax in sunshine/Olympics!

1.3 Listen to the candidate answering the question. Read the candidate's notes as you listen and underline the information you hear. What does the speaker forget to mention? Is any extra information added? What follow-up questions did the examiner ask?

D Make your own notes for the topic card in 5A. Remember you only have one minute in the exam. Then practise your talk with a partner. When you have finished, change roles.

6 Individual long turn

for this task

▸ Use the one minute preparation time to make notes and organise your thoughts before you speak.

▸ You will be asked to speak continuously for 1–2 minutes. Make sure your answer is relevant to each point on the card. You should try to cover each point on the card and make your ideas flow; connect them together in the order they appear on the topic card.

▸ Answer the examiner's round-off questions briefly.

Describe a sport or free-time activity that you enjoy doing.
You should say:
    what it is
    why you started doing it
    what it involves exactly
and explain why you enjoy doing it.

 In pairs practise the interview for 2–3 minutes.

Student A: You are the candidate. Use your notes to speak for 1–2 minutes. Follow the advice in the *for this task* box and the *express tip* boxes.

Student B: You are the examiner. Listen to Student A's answers carefully. Ask one or two brief questions to round off the candidate's long turn. Did he or she follow the advice in the *for this task* box and the *express tip* boxes?

When you have finished, change roles.

2 Education

LISTENING

▶ **Exam tasks** ▶ Form completion; multiple-choice questions with single answers
▶ **Exam focus** ▶ Listening Section 1: Non-academic dialogue
▶ **Skills** ▶ Anticipating what you will hear; following instructions carefully; identifying keywords and paraphrase

1 Introduction

A Look at the pictures above. What do they show? In what ways are they the same? How are they different?

B Look at the words in the box below. Which words relate to school education and which ones to university education? Which can relate to both? Discuss with a partner.

report	canteen	project	exams	term
seminar	coursework	tutor	uniform	pupil
assignment	lecture theatre	timetable	classroom	library

C Imagine you can hear the university students talking. Using the vocabulary above, discuss with a partner what they might be saying about:
- their daily study routines
- the university facilities
- the way they are assessed.

IN THE EXAM

Listening Section 1: Non-academic dialogue

The Listening module has four sections, with ten questions in each section. The Listening module takes around thirty minutes. You are then given a further ten minutes to transfer your answers to an answer sheet.

Section 1 of the Listening module is a non-academic dialogue with a transactional purpose. It features a conversation between two people in an everyday situation, such as buying goods or services, arranging a meeting or simply exchanging information. The conversation is approximately two minutes long and you will hear the recording once only.

Many different question types appear in this section, although there are some common types. In completion questions, you are presented with notes, a table or a form with information missing. You have to listen and fill in the gaps. Read the instructions carefully, as they will tell you the number of words you should use to complete your answer. In multiple-choice questions with single answers, you have to choose the most appropriate answer from a choice of three alternatives.

2 Anticipating what you will hear

One of the key strategies for success in the Listening module is to *anticipate* the situation and language you might hear. In this way, you are better prepared for the listening tasks that follow.

A Look at the form completion task below. With a partner, discuss:
- what the situation might be
- who the speakers might be
- where the conversation might take place
- what kind of topic-related language (vocabulary, questions and answers) you might hear.

Questions 1–6

Complete the form below. Write **NO MORE THAN THREE WORDS AND/OR A NUMBER** for each answer.

St. Vitus Academy
Course enrolment form

First Name:	1 _Sam_
Surname:	2 _Walker_
Address:	3 _____, London, N8 6BY
Age:	4 _____
Course:	5 _Modern dance_
Course Start Date:	6 _9th Sep_

In the Listening module, each section is given a short introduction, e.g. *You will hear two students talking about their favourite subjects.* Use this introduction to visualise the situation and *anticipate* the language you might hear.

 B **2.1** Listen to the introduction to the above form completion exercise. Did you predict the situation correctly?

 C **2.2** Now listen to the first part of the dialogue. Did you predict the location, language and speakers correctly?

In the exam you will be given some time to read the questions before you listen. Use this time to identify the type of information required for each answer.

D Look at Question 6 on the form. Is the answer a word, a number or a combination of the two? Can you make any predictions about the answer? Now look at questions 1–5 and do the same for each one.

 E **2.3** Listen to the whole recording and complete the form by answering questions 1–6.

3 Following instructions carefully

IELTS candidates can lose marks if they don't follow the instructions carefully. Typical errors are:

Type A using more than the specified number of words for an answer

Type B not using the actual words from the recording

Type C recording the answer in the wrong place

Look at the completed form below from 2A.

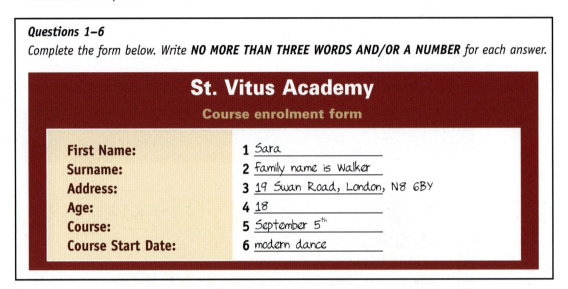

> *Questions 1–6*
>
> *Complete the form below. Write* **NO MORE THAN THREE WORDS AND/OR A NUMBER** *for each answer.*
>
> ### St. Vitus Academy
> #### Course enrolment form
>
> First Name: 1 Sara
> Surname: 2 Family name is Walker
> Address: 3 19 Swan Road, London, N8 6BY
> Age: 4 18
> Course: 5 September 5th
> Course Start Date: 6 modern dance

🎧 **2.3** The candidate has made some errors on the form. Listen to the recording again and mark the errors Type A, B or C on the form.

4 Identifying keywords and paraphrase

Multiple-choice questions are a common IELTS task type. You may be given the first half of a statement (known as the *stem*) and three alternative endings. To answer the question, choose the best option.

A Look at this multiple-choice question from the listening above.

> **1** The student wants a career as a(n)
>   **A** accountant.
>   **B** biologist.
>   **C** performer.

What is the keyword in the stem? Can you think of any synonyms or paraphrase for this keyword? Now look at the options. Can you think of any synonyms or paraphrase for these?

B You may hear information on the recording that relates to incorrect options. These 'distractors' are designed to test your ability to listen carefully.

🎧 **1** **2.4** Listen and make notes on what is said about the three options. What information is given about each option? How do we know which ones are distractors?

2 What is the answer to the multiple-choice question?

5 Form completion

 2.5 **Questions 1–7**

Complete the form below. Write **NO MORE THAN THREE WORDS** for each answer.

express tip

Don't always expect the keywords in the questions to be the same as on the recording – listen out for synonyms and paraphrase.

Jordan College, Oxford
Application form

COURSE: Business administration

PERSONAL DETAILS

First Name: Nigel ....

Surname: **1** ....

Date of Birth: **2** ....

Gender: Male ....

Country of Origin: U.K. ....

First Language: English ....

CONTACT DETAILS

Address: **3** ...., Oxford

Postcode: **4** ....

Tel.: 01865 **5** ....

'A' LEVEL QUALIFICATIONS

Maths: ..grade B ....

Economics: **6** ....

7 .... grade E

6 Multiple-choice questions with single answers

 2.6 **Questions 8–10**

Choose the correct letter, **A**, **B** or **C**.

8 The course code is
  A BA010. ✓
  B BA101.
  C BA011.

9 The course lasts
  A a month.
  ✓ **B** 9 months.
  C 12 months.

10 The nearest cashpoint is next to
  ✓ **A** the main lecture theatre.
  B the canteen.
  C the library.

▸ **Exam task** ▸ Describing graphs, bar charts, pie charts and tables
▸ **Exam focus** ▸ Academic Writing Task 1
▸ **Skills** ▸ Understanding visual information; writing the introduction; organising the main body text; comparing graphs

1 Introduction

Read the description of the UK and Australian higher education systems, then answer the questions below.

> In higher education institutions there are two levels of course: undergraduate and postgraduate. Students who graduate from an undergraduate course are awarded a degree dependent on their performance – in the UK the top classification is a 'first'; the lowest is a 'third'. Post-graduate courses lead to either a master's degree or a doctorate, also known as a 'PhD'.
>
> Generally, full-time undergraduate courses are three years long whilst postgraduate master courses last one year. In some subjects such as business, it is possible to enrol on a sandwich course, where a year of work experience in the middle of the course is 'sandwiched' between academic study.
>
> In both Australia and the UK many full-time students take on part-time jobs to help finance their studies and hopefully gain relevant work experience. This places greater pressure on students, who have to continually balance work and study commitments. However, many students give up working in their final year to concentrate on achieving a good degree to be able to compete in the challenging job market.

A What are the two levels of course you can study at university?
B What is the highest degree result you can achieve?
C What pressures are placed on students today?

With a partner, compare universities in the UK and Australia with the universities in your country.

IN THE EXAM

Academic Writing module: Task 1

The Academic Writing module consists of two tasks and takes one hour. As Task 1 provides one third of the total marks for the Writing module, it is advisable to spend no more than one third of your time on it (20 minutes).

In Task 1 of the Writing section you are expected to write a short descriptive report on visual information or data.

This visual information is most commonly presented in the form of statistical bar charts, pie charts or tables.

You are required to write at least 150 words and are assessed on the following: how well you address the question; how well your answer is organised (including how the information is linked together); vocabulary and sentence structure, including use of an appropriate academic style.

2 Understanding visual information

Study the graphs below and answer the following questions.
A Where does the information come from in each graph?
B What does the number and colour coding tell you in the key to Figure 1?
C What do the vertical and horizontal axes show in Figure 1?
D What do the numbers represent in Figure 2?
E Why do you think the total percentage in Figure 2 is not 100%?

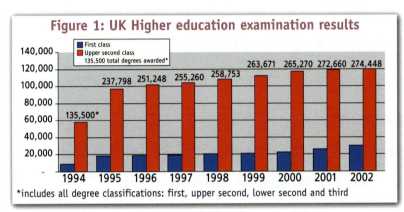

Source: *Times Higher Education Supplement*/Higher Education Statistics Agency

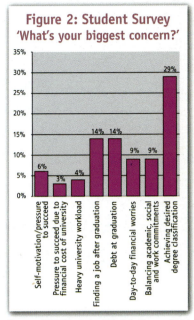

Source: *THES/Sodexho Lifestyle Survey 2004*

3 Writing the introduction

A Read the following introduction to a Task 1 report for Figure 1. Are the following statements about the introduction true (T) or false (F)?
1 It describes numbers within the chart.
2 It is based on information taken from the title, axes and key of the chart.

The bar chart illustrates higher education examination results in the UK from 1994 to 2002, showing the number of first and upper-second class degrees, as well as the total number of degrees awarded in each year within this period.

C Now write an introductory paragraph for Figure 2 using the model above as a guide.

4 Organising the main body text

A Having written an overview of the graph in the introduction, you should then summarise the key information in the main body text of the report.

1 Read the sentences below forming the first paragraph of the main-body text for the graph in Figure 2. Put the sentences in the correct order to form the main-body paragraph.

a *This concern was more than twice as important as finding a job after graduation and debt at graduation, which were jointly the second largest concerns for students.*

b *The first thing to note is that although students have many worries, their biggest one is achieving their desired degree classification.*

c *If you add up all these figures, it can be seen that these three concerns represent the biggest cause of anxiety for nearly half of all students.*

2 What do the underlined reference words in each sentence refer to?

B Read a student's notes below for the second paragraph of the main-body text.

• money – big worry for students (mentioned in three categories)
• joint third biggest concern

1 What are the three categories the student is referring to?
2 What is the total percentage for these three categories?
3 What categories represent the joint third biggest concern?

C Now write the second paragraph of the main body of text from the above notes.

5 Comparing graphs

A Study the pie charts below and discuss the following questions with a partner.
1 What do the pie charts show?
2 What key information in the charts can you compare?

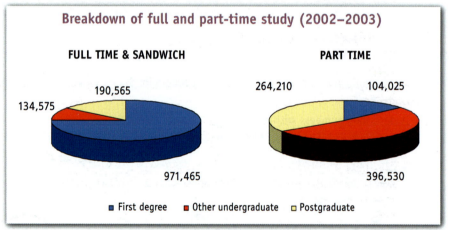

Breakdown of full and part-time study (2002–2003)

FULL TIME & SANDWICH — 190,565 — 134,575 — 971,465

PART TIME — 264,210 — 104,025 — 396,530

■ First degree   ■ Other undergraduate   □ Postgraduate

Source: Times Higher Education Supplement / Higher Education Statistics Agency

express tip

Structure your report: look first at the general perspective and then at specific detailed information.

B Read the description below relating to the information in the pie charts. Complete the gaps using words from the box to link the ideas together. Then finish the second paragraph in your own words.

| in terms of the figures | from an overall perspective | in comparison to |
| more specifically | the former | |

Looking at the pie charts **1** ...., the key information that stands out from a comparison of the two is that there were far more full-time and sandwich students than part-time students for the academic year 2002–2003. **2** .... there were approximately twice the number of **3** .... than the latter.

Looking at the pie charts **4** ...., the breakdown of different types of students was also very different for full-time students and sandwich students **5** .... part-timers.

C 1 Study the bar chart and table below and discuss with a partner what they show.

  2 Now write an introductory paragraph for a report outlining the information.

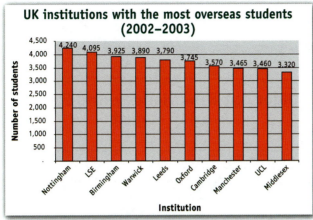

UK institutions with the most overseas students (2002–2003)

Source: *Times Higher Education Supplement*/British Council

UK institutions recording the greatest intake of foreign students (2002–2003)

	Numbers	% increase
Wolverhampton	2,720	159
Salford	1,735	72
Greenwich	2,110	63
Herts	2,480	61
Central Lancs	2,670	50
Portsmouth	1,960	46
Cardiff	2,620	46
Newcastle	2,290	44
London Met	3,165	41
Essex	2,215	40

Source: British Council

3 Look at the notes below. Write sentences comparing the following institutions in the chart and table to show some of the key information you could include in the main body of your report.

- *Nottingham/Wolverhampton*
- *Middlesex/all other institutions in bar chart*
- *Wolverhampton/Salford*
- *Nottingham/Middlesex*

6 Academic Writing Task 1: Report

for this task

- The data in this type of question may take the form of a graph, chart or table.

- Before you begin writing, spend a few minutes taking in and interpreting the factual information. Follow this writing process: think, plan, write.

- Write a brief introduction in your own words using information from the question and the headings in a table or axis in a graph, etc. Don't simply copy the wording in the exam question – use a variety of language: *the graph/chart/table illustrates/shows a breakdown/presents*, etc.

- Divide the main body of your essay into two or three paragraphs describing the key information in the table/chart/graph. The first main body paragraph should list your main points, which should be supported with evidence. Secondary points and observations regarding surprising or interesting information should follow in subsequent paragraphs (and contrast with your main points if possible).

- In the exam, you might be asked to describe two graphs or diagrams. If this is the case, you need to compare and contrast the information and make connections between the two. Use the language of comparisons to compare different statistics: *more/less numerous than, twice as many as, double, a fraction of*, etc.

You should spend about 20 minutes on this task.

The table below shows the average band scores for students from different language groups taking the IELTS Academic Paper in 2003.

Summarise the information by selecting and reporting the main features, and make comparisons where relevant.

Write at least 150 words.

	Listening	Reading	Writing	Speaking	Overall
Hindi	6.78	6.38	6.62	6.86	6.73
Malayalam	6.31	6.13	6.49	6.52	6.43
Russian	6.35	6.13	6.11	6.69	6.38
Spanish	6.27	6.42	6.08	6.64	6.41

Source: www.ielts.org

Questions 1–5

Complete the table below.

Write **NO MORE THAN THREE WORDS AND/OR A NUMBER** *for each answer.*

Oldbridge Bank Holiday Arts Festival
31ˢᵗ August

	Old Bus Station (example) Arts Centre	Town Hall	Lincoln Park
2:00–4:00	'Uncle Spoon and the 1 .... Balloon' Children's theatre	'Chasing Clouds' 2 .... readings	Nick Goose Folk singer
5:00– 3	Storytelling workshop	'First Steps' New short plays	Trad Dad and the Modern All Stars 4 .... band
8:00–late	'Gypsy Ballads' 5 .... dance	Eddie Hicks Stand up comedy	Maidenhead Heavy metal band

Questions 6–8

Complete the form below.

Write **NO MORE THAN THREE WORDS AND/OR A NUMBER** for each answer.

Ticket Application Form

Name:	6 ....Simon Evans.......
Address:	7 .....Bradford way....., Oldbridge
Telephone number:	8 .....9300 1384.....

Questions 9–10

Choose the correct letter **A**, **B** or **C**.

9   The price of an ordinary ticket to see all the events is
   A   £12.
   B   £20.
   C   £25.

10   The caller found out about the festival through
   A   advertising in the street.
   B   entertainment listings in a local newspaper.
   C   word of mouth.

Natural Rubber
An exotic material

A Today, we take modern materials very much for granted, without knowing their origin or realising their versatility. Rubber for example, is a vital component of cars, supplying traction between the wheels and the road, as well as sealing oil and fuel from leakage and absorbing unwanted vibrations from the engine. Rubber also supplies us with many domestic items (toy balloons, water bottles, condoms, carpet underlay, mattresses and cushioning), office products (rubber bands, erasers) and articles of sports and recreation (footballs, golf balls, tennis balls, etc.). But where does rubber come from?

B Natural rubber was discovered during the various invasions of South America by the Spanish conquistadors in the 15th century. The material, made simply by drying out the sap of a native tree, *Hevea brasiliensis*, was first spotted by Columbus in the West Indies in the 1490s, where it was used to make balls. It was also made into bags for carrying liquids by moulding flexible rubber sheet into the desired shape. Rubber was clearly a material well known to native cultures, and recent discoveries of its use in ancient ceremonies are hardly surprising.

C Despite its early discovery by the Spanish, it was not until about 1730 that rubber was introduced into Britain, and not until 1791 that its use for the mackintosh (the rubberised raincoat) was introduced. In 1770 Joseph Priestley, who also discovered oxygen, noticed that rubber erases pencil marks. Despite this serendipitous finding, it still took some time before the material was to find widespread application. One reason for this was its deterioration with time, degrading in air to a sticky unmanageable mess. That was to change dramatically with the invention of 'vulcanization', when, in 1834, Charles Goodyear found that cooking the material with raw sulphur stabilised it and stiffened products manufactured from the substance.

D This discovery opened the way to pneumatic tyres for early vehicles such as carriages, (travel in which was rather painful owing to the rigid wheels and rough roads then in existence). The first patent for a tyre dates from 1846, when Robert Thompson announced the pneumatic tyre, a great advance for wheeled traffic. The key to the idea is the cushion provided by the air pocket, the pressure of which can be varied to suit the user. The invention languished, perhaps because of problems with containing the inevitable leaks of air from the many inner tubes. However, solid rubber tyres were subsequently adopted, with much reduced cushioning.

E At the same time, vulcanized rubber came to be used for an increasing number of products, such as galoshes or Wellington boots and improved mackintoshes, where rubber was combined with textile to make a waterproof fabric. The growing demand for natural rubber made it a commodity product, yet only supplied by one area in the world – Brazil. As a result, the price soared, creating rich entrepreneurs, who essentially exploited natives to collect the raw latex from the rainforest. But since the tree could potentially be grown in any tropical climate, why not collect seedlings and transplant to other countries?

F Intensive efforts were made at Kew Gardens to raise healthy plants from seeds collected by Sir Henry Wickham in Brazil in 1876. The young trees raised in the tropical greenhouse at Kew were shipped to Ceylon and Malaysia to form the nucleus of large plantations. Those countries were able to meet the rising demands of the rubber industry, and the price of raw rubber fell dramatically.

G In 1888, over forty years after Thompson's invention of the pneumatic tyre, John Dunlop, a Belfast vet, responded to a request from his young son for better tyres for his trike. When ridden over the rough cobbles of Belfast's streets, solid rubber tyres just could not give a comfortable ride. Various rubber tubes were used by vets, and Dunlop re-invented the pneumatic tyre by fitting a wheel with an inflated rubber tube protected by a heavier outer cover. After much experimentation, the world's first bicycle tyre emerged.

H Dunlop's first patent to protect the invention was inevitably invalid because of Thompson's prior patent, but he went on to invent the valve and numerous other components which were proved valid. Those inventions were the base on which he and others built the bike tyre industry, which brought cycling into a new era for everyone. It was an era when industrial progress had created new-found wealth and leisure time for millions. As with any new and fundamental invention, the idea was taken up by others, in particular by Michelin in France (1896), to develop a much heavier-duty device, the car tyre.

I Today a wide range of synthetic rubber is available to designers, many for specialty tasks requiring, for example, very high or low temperatures. Yet natural rubber is still a valuable international commodity, helping many developing countries earn useful hard currency. The technology of processing the raw rubber has improved greatly over the years, but the basics still remain the same as they were when Kew Gardens selected the best plants for cloning and transplanting over one hundred years ago.

Source: The Open University

Questions 1–8

*The reading passage has nine paragraphs **A–I**.*

*Choose the correct heading for paragraphs **B–I** from the list of headings below.*

*Write the correct number **i–xii** next to question numbers 1–8.*

List of Headings

i	The future of rubber
ii	Useful additions to an existing idea
iii	How to grow a rubber tree
iv	Useful for making your coat waterproof
v	The first known uses
vi	Exporting new forests
vii	Inspiration from a bumpy bicycle ride
viii	How different is rubber nowadays?
ix	New demand leads to dramatically escalating cost
x	Unpopular due to decay
xi	A good idea in principle
xii	Many modern uses

Example	Answer
Paragraph **A**	**xii**

1 Paragraph **B**   .....   5 Paragraph **F**   .....

2 Paragraph **C**   .....   6 Paragraph **G**   .....

3 Paragraph **D**   .....   7 Paragraph **H**   .....

4 Paragraph **E**   .....   8 Paragraph **I**   .....

Questions 9–13

Complete the summary below using words from the box.

Dunlop's comfortable tyre

Dunlop originally devised a new tyre to make his son's trike more comfortable. He was familiar with different types of rubber as he used them in his **9** .... A lighter inner tube filled with air was fitted inside a heavier rubber **10** .... Unfortunately, he could not patent it due to a **11** .... between his and an earlier invention. It was the **12** .... of the valve which proved his success. Around this time people had more **13** .... and so cycling was taken up by the masses.

water	match	city	tube	supplement
difference	subtraction	transport	life	oxygen
practice √	money	addition	casing	similarity

Questions 14–16

Answer the questions below using **NO MORE THAN THREE WORDS** *for each answer.*

14 What is the name of the method which prevents rubber from deteriorating?
15 What happened when the demand for rubber greatly outstripped supply?
16 In which tropical countries were the new supplies of rubber trees grown?

▶ WRITING TASK 1

You should spend about 20 minutes on this task.

The table below shows a breakdown of companies advertising expenditure in different media sectors in three countries (Australia, South Korea and Brazil).

Summarise the information by selecting and reporting the main features, and make comparisons where relevant.

Write at least 150 words.

Advertising expenditure breakdown (%)

	Australia	Korea	Brazil
TV	25	27	61
Newspaper	23	22	16
Radio	21	21	14
Internet	15	6	3
Sponsorship	8	12	5
Direct Mail	8	12	1

SPEAKING

PART 1
Example questions
• Have you travelled far to come here today?
• How would you describe your local area?
• What's the best thing about the area where you live?
• What is your favourite part of the city?

PART 2
Example task
Read the topic card below carefully.
You will have to talk about the topic for one to two minutes.
You have one minute to think about what you are going to say.
You can make notes to help you if you wish.

> **Describe one possession you could not live without.**
> **You should say:**
>   **what the object is**
>   **how often you use it**
>   **what you would do if you lost it**
> **and explain why it is so important to you.**

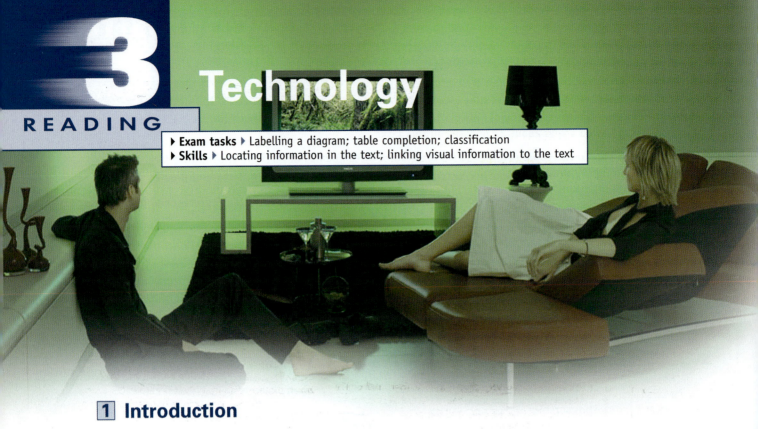

3 Technology

READING

> **Exam tasks** ▸ Labelling a diagram; table completion; classification
> **Skills** ▸ Locating information in the text; linking visual information to the text

1 Introduction

Discuss these questions with a partner.
- What was the last hi-tech product you bought? Are you satisfied with it? Has it changed a particular aspect of your life? If so, how?
- Would you classify yourself as a technophile or a technophobe? Why?

2 Locating information in the text

A Skim the passage opposite and match the paragraph summaries to the correct paragraph.

Paragraph 1   **a** Product range and pros of both models
Paragraph 2   **b** Internet-enabled functions of PDAs
Paragraph 3   **c** Pros and cons of the PALM MASTER
Paragraph 4   **d** Introduction
Paragraph 5   **e** Pros and cons of the ZV

B Look at the table opposite comparing two PDAs. In which paragraph in the passage would you expect to find each answer?

Before you complete the table, you need to decide what information is needed. To help you, match a–e below with 1–5 in the table.

a another advantage of the PALM MASTER   ......
b something missing from the PALM MASTER   ......
c something built into the ZV   ......
d something not up to standard on the ZV   ......
e something which doesn't fit in the restricted space   ......

IN THE EXAM

The Reading module: question types

There are three main groups of question types in the Reading module: matching tasks such as classification or matching headings to paragraphs; gap-fill tasks such as table completion, summary completion, labelling a diagram and sentence completion; selection tasks such as multiple choice or true/false/not given, where the answer is simply a choice from the selection.

Homework

READING

PDA* model	Positive features	Negative features
Informatica ZV POCKET	• Integrated 1 .... *wi-Fi* • Full range of multimedia features	• Poor quality 2 .... *cammera* • Limited 3 .... *memory* storage
Techzone PALM MASTER	• Good compatibility with Microsoft Office™ software • 4 .... *sharp clear screen*	• Limited range of multimedia features • No 5 ....

*PDA: personal digital assistant, also known as an 'electronic organiser' or a 'palm-top' computer

C Read the mini text on PDAs and complete the table, using no more than three words for each answer.

express tip

Some reading texts provide explanations of difficult words in footnotes. These words are indicated in the text with an asterisk (*).

In the palm of your hand

1 We've tested two very different PDAs (personal digital assistants) this issue: Informatica's latest all-singing, all-dancing ZV POCKET PC and the new Techzone PALM MASTER.

2 The ZV comes with built-in Wi-Fi* to accommodate people's mobile lifestyles, as well as comprehensive multimedia functions. The drawbacks, however, are the 1.3 megapixel digital camera which disappoints, as does the restricted memory for storing music and video files: an iPod® it isn't.

3 The PALM MASTER on the other hand, although lacking in multimedia functionality and not wireless-enabled as standard, does provide a solid choice for professionals who want good compatibility with Microsoft Office™ software and a sharp clear screen to view data. The main downside is perhaps the absence of a docking station for easy connection to your PC.

4 Unlike the ZV, the PALM MASTER is not part of a very broad product range – with the ZV, you can choose from a variety of models which are aimed at different types of users. The top of the range ZV, for example, amazingly incorporates biometric security which protects data from theft or duplication using the owner's unique fingerprint. All in all though, both models boast fast processors, cutting edge design and bundled software to provide good value for money. It is worth noting though that the Techzone tends to be more competitively priced.

5 Whether you buy the PALM MASTER or the ZV, you'll need to arrange a remote Internet connection to exploit all the functions and features of these products – PDAs have come a long way from the days of being simply electronic diaries. You can send emails, prepare a presentation or do a spreadsheet, but if you don't care to do all this on a miniature keyboard, then the ZV will appeal with the chance to purchase a snap-on full-size foldable keyboard as an optional extra. Now, there really is no excuse not to work whilst travelling!

*a function on a lap-top or palm-top computer to provide connection to the Internet when mobile.

D Look at the classification exercise below. Answer the following questions and then complete the exercise.

1 Why is it a good idea to scan for keywords in the statements rather than the names of the categories? Discuss with a partner.

2 Locate the keywords or paraphrased words in the text which correspond to the keywords highlighted in bold in the statements. Underline the relevant sections of the text.

Classify the following statements as referring to

A INFORMATICA ZV
B Techzone PALM MASTER
C Both

1 **Internet access** is essential to fully take advantage of the product. ......
2 The product is **not over-priced**. ......
3 It provides **a wide choice of models.** ......
4 It is possible to buy **add-on accessories**. ......
5 It is not simple to connect to your **desktop computer**. ......

UNIT 3 Technology **31**

3 Linking visual information to the text

A Look at the diagram of a conventional television. Explain how it might work to your partner.

B Skim the passage below and locate the paragraph section that describes the diagram.

C Look at the labels on the diagram and answer the following questions.
  1 In which direction are the labels arranged?
  2 What type of answer is needed in Labels 1 and 2 – a noun, verb, adverb or adjective?

D Read the relevant section of the passage again and complete the diagram. Use a maximum of three words for each answer, taken directly from the passage.

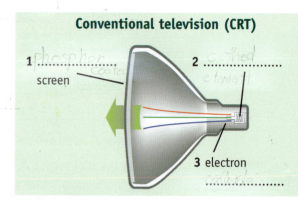

Conventional television (CRT)

1 .... screen

2 ....

3 electron

....

The Future is Flat

Plummeting prices and ultra cool design of new flat-panel TVs are spelling the end of the conventional TV.

The panels are flat but the sales most certainly aren't. The television market, long dominated by the conventional TV, is undergoing a revolution. The 'tube' or the 'box' as it is often known, sits heavily in the corner of most living rooms across the planet. Beautiful, it isn't. But that's about to change if sales forecasts are realised. Already millions of families are opting for thin-screen wall-mountable plasmas and LCD TVs as the latest consumer product of choice.

Statistics show that Americans watch TV on average for four hours a day, whilst Europeans watch three hours, so it's not surprising that consumers are saying that as they spend so much time watching TV, that they might as well look at something that looks good! But it's not just viewing statistics that are impressive; the economic statistics are also looking good, with the market for thin-screen TVs worth $21 billion in 2004. Plasmas are taking the biggest slice of this market, especially for screens of 40 inches or more where they have an 88% slice of the market. LCDs are also selling fast, but relative to plasmas the growth rate is slower.

The end looks to be in sight for the conventional CRT TV, although for now, Cathode-ray-tube (CRT) televisions still account for 72% of US sales. This is perhaps not surprising if you think that they have been around for over fifty years. With bargain prices starting from $100 and having an extremely long life expectancy, CRTs are not going to disappear overnight. The downside of course is that they are big and bulky and are unlikely to win any design awards. The technology though, is tried and tested – all colour televisions create images using red, green and blue light, but conventional televisions use an electron gun to generate these images. The cathode element within the gun emits beams of electrons which are fired at a phosphor-coated screen which is covered with blue, green and red phosphors. The larger the screen, the longer the tube needed and the bigger the box.

At present, demand for plasma TVs is overtaking that of LCDs, as prices are 10% to 20% cheaper for similar-sized screens, although this price differential is narrowing. Plasmas also beat LCDs in terms of maximum screen size, offering consumers an almost cinema-like experience with screen sizes ranging up to a massive 55 inches (137.5cm) with models such as Hitachi's PD5200. Plasmas also don't suffer from the problem of trailing edge blur with fast-moving images, which is the problem with even the best LCDs on the market. Having said that, they have had some problems with image burn-in that leaves static images on the screen, like permanent ghost images. This is not so much of an issue as you might think as this is only likely to occur when the same image, such as a sign, is continuously displayed on screen. Since TV images are constantly in motion, burn-in isn't likely to be a problem so long as the screen isn't hooked up to your computer and used as a PC monitor.

LCDs, on the other hand, win hands down in terms of weight, slimness and flexibility – they can be as little as 4cm thick (Toshiba 20VL56) compared to 8–15cm for plasmas, they are more durable and weigh considerably less than their plasma equivalent, and can also be easily wall-mounted. Over the life of the product, a strong case can be made for the cost efficiency of LCDs, as they have a life expectancy of 25 years (that's at least 10 years more than plasmas) and will cost you far less for extended warranties – three-year warranties on plasmas typically start at $400 whilst for LCDs the equivalent screen size model would cost you around $150.

So, how does the technology work? Plasma screens are made up of a mesh of tiny light bulbs with each bulb filled with electrically ionised gas which glows red, green or blue. LCDs, on the other hand, are transmissive devices with screens consisting of white fluorescent light which is shone through up to a million pixels depending on the resolution of the screen. Each pixel contains liquid crystal cells with tiny micro-transistors behind them, which are turned on and off by a signal from a computer to vary the intensity of the light. This light is in turn sent through RGB filters to create the correctly coloured pixel image on the front glass screen.

The big picture then for consumers and retailers alike is that plasma and LCD TVs are today's high-tech tubes and as new players enter the market so quality and value for money will rise further. Plasmas look the better buy for the present, but LCDs are likely to seize market share in the future when screen sizes get bigger and prices come down. This trend will be further accelerated with the expected entry into the market of the big PC manufacturers, offering even lower prices together with technological innovation.

4 Labelling a diagram

express tip

Focus not just on *what* the answer is but also on *where* the answer is. If you can find the answer quickly (using skimming and scanning techniques), you can answer it quickly.

for this task

▶ Locate the section of the text that refers to the diagram, then read it in detail to ensure you fully understand it. Pay particular attention to locate specific words that form part of the labels in the diagram.

▶ When completing the label, be aware of grammatical connections – some words are correct in terms of meaning but do not fit grammatically.

▶ Unless you are given a vocabulary box with a list of words to choose from, make sure you take words directly from the text – do not try to think of synonyms. Whether you are given the words or you need to locate them in the text, ensure that you copy them correctly to avoid spelling mistakes.

▶ Keep in mind that labels on the diagram are generally ordered in a clockwise direction, which will not necessarily reflect the order the information appears in the passage.

Questions 1–5

Label the diagram below.

Choose **NO MORE THAN THREE WORDS** from the reading passage for each answer.

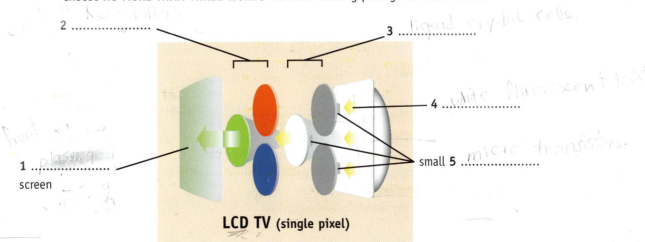

2 ....

3 ....

4 ....

1 ....
screen

small 5 ....

LCD TV (single pixel)

5 Table completion

for this task

▸ Take a moment to look at the rows and columns of the table to understand how the information is organised and what is required to answer each question before consulting the passage for the answer.

▸ Scan for keywords or paraphrases from the table in the passage. Sometimes the information is located in one place in the passage, other times the information is distributed across the whole passage.

▸ Make sure you use exact words and phrases from the text – do not try to use words that do not appear in the text as these will be marked wrong even if the meaning is correct.

▸ Follow the instructions carefully, especially regarding the maximum number of words permitted in the answer – normally no more than three.

Questions 6–12

Label the table below.

Choose **NO MORE THAN THREE WORDS AND/OR A NUMBER** from the passage on pages 32 and 33 for each answer.

	CRT	Plasma	LCD
Economic picture	6 .... market share in US	7 .... market share (large screens)	8 .... not as fast compared to plasmas
Downside	Big and bulky	Ghost images 9	High prices at present
Upside	Very low 10	Very large 11	Light-weight, slim and can be 12 ....

6 Classification

for this task

▸ For this question type you will need to match a list of statements to a particular category.

▸ The categories will be listed in an order, usually chronological or alphabetical, so the statements will probably not match the order in which they are mentioned in the passage.

▸ Decide whether to scan for keywords in the statements

or for the names of categories. Your decision should be based on the frequency of the keyword. If the word appears frequently, it is pointless scanning for it as it will appear throughout the passage.

▸ Often, there is more than one statement in the question that has a connection with the category, but only one statement will match it exactly.

Questions 13–18

Classify the following facts as referring to

A CRTs

B LCDs

C Plasmas

13 Computer companies will shortly manufacture this type of TV. ....
14 They are relatively light and last a long time. ....
15 Blurring of fast moving images occurs on this type of TV. ....
16 They offer the best value for money flat-screen TV at the moment. ....
17 They are the most bulky type of TV. ....
18 They are becoming relatively less expensive. ....

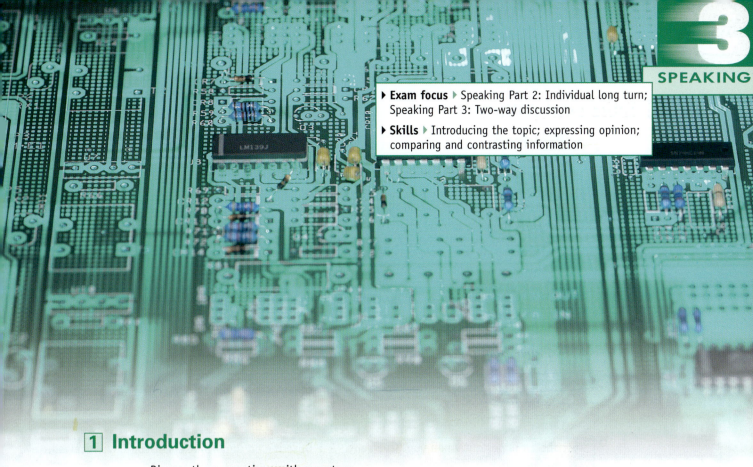

▶ **Exam focus** ▶ Speaking Part 2: Individual long turn;
Speaking Part 3: Two-way discussion

▶ **Skills** ▶ Introducing the topic; expressing opinion;
comparing and contrasting information

1 | Introduction

Discuss these questions with a partner.
- How does modern technology improve the quality of our lives?
- What negative effects can technology have on our lives? Consider work, family, transport and education.

2 | Introducing the topic

 A **3.1** Listen to four candidates taking Part 2 of the Speaking module. Make notes and identify the correct topic question from the list below.

      1 Describe a machine or device which is important to you.

      2 Describe an important email which you sent or received.

      3 Describe an email you sent by mistake.

 B **3.1** Listen again. What language do the candidates use to introduce their talks?

C Look at the language for introducing your talk in the box below.

> OK then, I want to talk about ...
> Let me see, I'd like to talk about ...
>
> OK, I'm going to tell you about ...
> Right, I'd like to tell you about ...

express tip

In the exam, try to sound confident; begin your talk without hesitating.

Using the language in the box above and the notes you made in 2A, practise introducing the talk to a partner.

IN THE EXAM

Speaking module: Parts 2 and 3

In Part 2 of the Speaking exam you are given a card showing a number of points relating to a particular topic. You will be asked to talk about the subject on the card for 1–2 minutes. The examiner will expect you to cover all the points in your answer.

Part 3 is an extended two-way discussion with the examiner. The topic will be thematically linked to Part 2, but you will talk about things in a more abstract way. For example, if you spoke about sending an email in Part 2, in Part 3 you may be asked about how technology has affected the way we communicate.

A

3 Individual long turn

for this task

▸ Make notes to help you talk about the topic on your card, including vocabulary you want to include.

▸ Keep your answer relevant to the instructions on the card and try to address each point in turn.

▸ Introduce your topic with confidence, using appropriate language.

Work with a partner. In pairs, role-play Part 2 of the Speaking exam.

Student A: You are the candidate. For one minute, look at Topic Card A below and make notes. Use your notes to help you speak for 1–2 minutes. Follow the advice in the *for this task* box above.

Student B: You are the examiner. Give Student A one minute to look at Topic Card A and make notes. Then listen to Student A's answer carefully. Does he or she follow the advice in the *for this task* box? After 1–2 minutes, interrupt Student A and ask one or two questions to round off the long turn.

When you have finished, change roles, this time using Topic Card B.

> **express tip**
>
> Make notes quickly as you only have one minute to do this in the exam. Don't write full sentences, just note down key points and vocabulary.

Topic Card A

> Describe an important email you have sent.
> You should say:
> who the email was to
> what it was about
> if you got a reply
> and explain why the email was important.

Topic Card B

> Describe an important email you have received.
> You should say:
> who the email was from
> what it was about
> if you sent a reply
> and explain why the email was important.

4 Expressing opinion

> **express tip**
>
> Don't always justify your answer using *because*. In natural English we often don't use conjunctions at all: *I think email is great; it's cheap, quick and global.*

A Here are some possible questions from Part 3 of the Speaking module, relating to the topic in Part 2 above. Discuss the questions with a partner, giving reasons for your opinions.

1 Do you think technology has changed the way we communicate?

2 How do job opportunities differ for those who have computer-related skills from those who do not?

3 Do you think the existence of computers in schools has improved the way students learn?

B Now answer these questions.

1 How many of the opinions expressed by your partner can you remember? What reasons were given to justify his or her opinions?

2 What language was used to introduce his/her opinion?

C 3.2 Now listen to seven students answering the same questions. What language do they use to introduce their opinions? Tick (✔) the boxes.

In my view …	❑	I reckon …	❑	I guess …	❑
I doubt …	❑	Personally, I think …	❑	I'm (not) sure if …	❑
To my mind …	❑	I (don't) think …	❑	In my opinion …	❑
I believe …	❑	I suppose …	❑	For me …	❑

D Practise asking and answering the questions in 4A with different students, using as many different ways of expressing your opinion as you can.

5 Comparing and contrasting information

A In the exam you can make comparisons in order to justify your opinion. Use language to describe the similarities and differences between two things in order to contrast them.

Look at the following example answer. What language is used to show a comparison?

'When we get to work, there can be lots of emails to respond to, so I suppose in some ways email is also more time-consuming than before.'

B ● **3.3** Listen to some candidates justifying their opinions and complete the sentences. Then underline any language useful for making comparisons.

1 Email is much .... and .... writing a letter. In some ways, email is also .... before.

2 Going to a library and using the Internet .... they are both great sources of information. The Internet is fantastic, but it's .... going to a library. I suppose .... you can hold a book.

3 I use mine all the time. ...., they are expensive. My bill last month was $100, ... normal phone calls are ....

4 Training people is expensive in the short term; ...., it will eventually benefit the national economy.

C Work with a partner to form comparison sentences from these notes, using the structures in 5B.

1 communicating by email/telephone/letter/videophone/text (SMS) messaging
2 travelling by train/plane/car/motorbike/bicycle/walking
3 'traditional' banking/banking online
4 doing research using books/using the Internet
5 'traditional' shopping/shopping online

6 Two-way discussion

for this task

▸ Introduce your opinion in different ways, don't just say, 'I think …'. Justify your opinion with a reason or example.

▸ If you cannot think of an answer immediately, buy yourself some time by saying, 'That's a good question'.

▸ Don't wait for the examiner to prompt you to speak, take the initiative and add extra information yourself.

▸ When you expand your idea, you can compare things. Talk about similarities and differences.

In pairs practise the two-way discussion for 4–5 minutes using the list of questions below.

Student A: You are the examiner. Ask Student B questions from the list. Don't forget to ask follow-up questions for each one. Listen to Student B's answers carefully. Did he or she express and justify his or her opinions? What language was used to introduce opinions? Were comparisons made?

Student B: You are the candidate. Listen to your partner's questions and answer them as fully as possible. Don't forget to justify your opinions. Do the questions require you to make a comparison?

When you have finished, change roles.

Questions
▸ Do you think children and old people have different attitudes towards technology?
▸ Board games are being replaced by video games. Is this having an effect on families?
▸ Have attitudes towards using the Internet for shopping changed in your country since it became widely available?

---

express tip

It will help you in the exam if you have a general knowledge of current affairs. Stay up-to-date with the news. Ask yourself: *What do I think? Why do I think it?*

4 The Workplace

▶ **Exam tasks** ▶ Flowchart completion; label completion
▶ **Exam focus** ▶ Listening Section 2: Non-academic monologue
▶ **Skills** ▶ Identifying signpost words; following a description

1 Introduction

Discuss these questions with a partner.
- In what types of places do people work?
- What are the advantages and disadvantages of some of these workplaces?
- In what type of workplace would you prefer to work? Give reasons for your answer.

2 Identifying signpost words

A The flowchart below shows a company's procedure for booking meeting rooms.

1 Study the flowchart. How many stages are there? Try to get a general idea of how the process works.

2 Now read the extract from a talk explaining the same procedure. With a partner, predict words or phrases suitable for gaps a–d. Don't worry about the blocked out words at this stage.

How to book meeting rooms

> Select type of room, time and **1** ....

↓

> Complete booking form with your **2** ....

↓

> Receive confirmation by **3** ....

> We ask everybody to follow this simple room-booking procedure using the company intranet. **a** ...., choose the sort of room you require and, most importantly, don't forget to tell us the time and ▮▮▮▮▮▮▮ you'll be needing it. **b** .... you might also like to let us know if you have any special requirements – conference calling facilities, for example. Coffee and other refreshments are always available. But if you need sandwiches, a buffet or a sit-down lunch, you need to contact the catering department. **c** ...., fill in the booking form with your ▮▮▮▮▮▮▮ . This is an internal billing requirement, so please don't forget. **d** ...., you'll get confirmation of your room booking via ▮▮▮▮▮▮▮ . And that's it! Simple!

 3 **4.1** Now listen to the recording. Check your answers to Questions a–d. Some words have been removed.

IN THE EXAM

Listening Section 2: Non-academic monologue

Section 2 of the IELTS listening exam is a non-academic monologue of a social nature, usually a person giving a talk about an everyday subject.

As with all IELTS listening tasks, you will hear this section only once. Many different question types may appear, including flowchart completion, labelling a diagram or map, and multiple-choice questions.

B Answers a–d are signpost words; they help to show how sections of a text link together.

1 Look at the correct answers to a–d. Put them into the correct category of signpost word.

Function	Signpost word
Listing	lastly, ...
Adding	in addition, ...
Sequencing	after, ...

20
20
20

2 Can you think of any more signpost words? Add them to the list.

3 Read the extract again, pointing to the relevant stage in the flowchart. Which signpost words move you on to the next stage?

C For each gap in the flowchart, identify the keywords and the answer type required, as well as any synonyms or paraphrases that might help you predict the answer.

D **4.2** Listen to the complete talk and fill in the flowchart. Use no more than three words for each answer.

3 Following a description

A Look at the diagram below.

1 How are the gaps 1–3 arranged? Left to right? Anti-clockwise?

2 How many words can you use for each answer?

3 Describe the diagram to yourself. You will often be given a starting reference point. Where is each part of the desk in relation to this reference point? Where are they in relation to each other?

4 What do you think the missing word(s) might be? Are there any keywords to help you?

B **4.3** Label the diagram. Write no more than three words for each answer.

The Mobile Office

> **express tip**
> Some parts of a diagram may have complete labels. Use these as markers to help you follow the explanation.

heavy-duty **1** ...*antistip*... rubber   optional **2** ...*storage*... pencil drawer

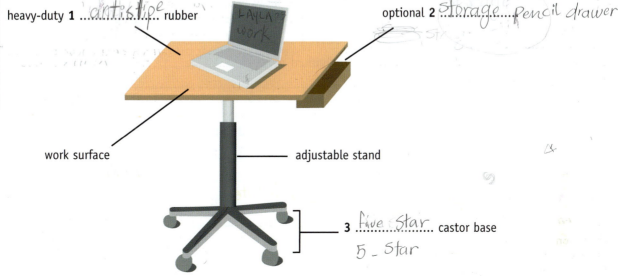

work surface   adjustable stand

3 ...*five star*... castor base

5 - Star

UNIT 4   The Workplace   **39**

4 Flowchart completion

for this task

Flowchart completion questions are answered by filling in the gaps with words from the recording.

Before you listen

▶ Study the sequence of stages. Predict what kind of information you are likely to hear on the recording.

▶ For each question identify the keyword(s), any synonyms or paraphrases, and the answer type. Try to predict the answer.

As you listen

▶ Listen for signpost words indicating a move to the next stage.

▶ Listen for keywords and paraphrases. When you hear them, the answer will be close by.

▶ Remember to use the exact words you hear in your answer, anything else will be marked incorrect.

After you listen

Check your spelling and ensure you haven't exceeded the word limit for any answer.

4.4 *Questions 1–6*

Complete the flow chart below.

*Write **NO MORE THAN THREE WORDS** for each answer.*

Recruitment Process

Candidates given a **1** ......group...... exercise.

↓

Candidates give a short **2** ......presaintion ✗
presentation

↓

Role-play exercise

↓

Psychometric tests to analyse candidates' **3** ......mental proces

↓

Individual **4** ......to be alone ✗ interview.

↓

After assessment, successful candidate is **5** ......offered the position.

↓

references. ✗ **6** ......Candidate...... are taken up.

express tip

Signpost words tell you when the speaker is moving on to a new idea or stage. Listen out for them!

5 Label completion

for this task

Label completion questions present you with a map or diagram. Some parts are labelled, others are not. You are required to fill in the gaps in the labels with no more than a specified number of words. You may be asked to complete a whole label or only part of it.

Before you listen

▸ Note how the label numbers are arranged. Identify any parts which are already labelled. Where is each part in relation to the others?

▸ Partially completed labels offer you keywords to listen out for. Can you predict any answers?

As you listen

▸ Listen carefully for references to any part of the map or diagram which is already labelled. Use these as your starting reference point or as 'markers' to prevent you getting lost.

▸ Listen carefully for words describing position (*on the left, above, below* etc). Point to each part of the map/diagram as it is described.

▸ Listen for any keywords, focusing more on the labels than on the diagram. Write each answer as you hear it.

After you listen

Check your spelling and the number of words you have used for each answer.

 4.5 *Questions 1–5*

Label the diagram below.

Write **NO MORE THAN TWO WORDS** *for each answer.*

The Logo Machine

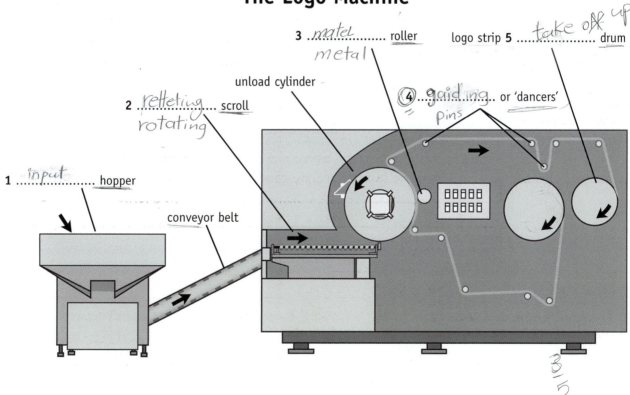

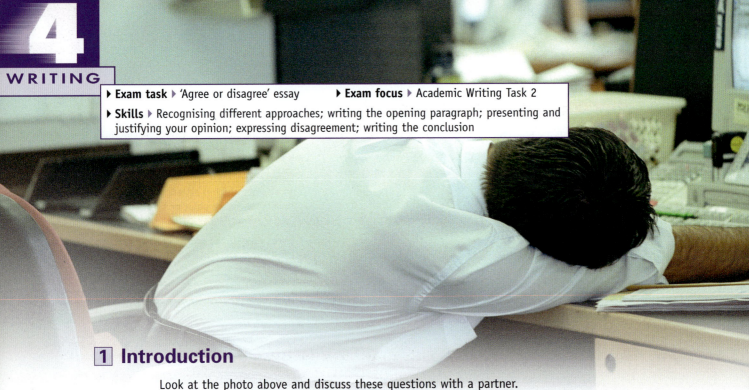

4 WRITING

> **Exam task** ▶ 'Agree or disagree' essay ▶ **Exam focus** ▶ Academic Writing Task 2
> ▶ **Skills** ▶ Recognising different approaches; writing the opening paragraph; presenting and justifying your opinion; expressing disagreement; writing the conclusion

1 Introduction

Look at the photo above and discuss these questions with a partner.
- How do you think this person feels about his job?
- Are some jobs more satisfying than others?
- What factors do you think lead to job satisfaction?

2 Recognising different approaches

Read the Task 2 exam question. Then read the two introductions below answering the question. How are they similar? How do they differ? Discuss with a partner.

> **Schools do not teach the skills that students require once they leave school to establish a career. Only subjects applicable to the workplace should be taught at school.**
>
> **To what extent do you agree or disagree with this opinion?**

A School subjects are varied and cover a number of areas such as science, humanities and the arts. However, much of what is learnt is useless once children leave school, while many other important skills are not taught at all. I believe that schools should only teach the subjects and skills that will be beneficial once students enter the workforce and adult life.

B School subjects are varied and cover a number of areas such as science, humanities and the arts. Much of what is learnt is not always directly relevant to real life. But is our time in full-time education only meant to teach us skills for the workforce, or can it be argued that education has a wider purpose?

IN THE EXAM

Academic writing module: Task 2

In Writing Task 2 you are presented with an argument, an opinion or a problem. Some questions ask you: *How far do you agree?* or: *To what extent do you agree?* This type of 'agree or disagree' question does not require you to discuss both sides of the issue, so you can use a thesis-led approach.

If you have a clear opinion on the subject, you may decide to use this approach. When using a thesis-led approach, you should state your opinion clearly in the introduction and use subsequent paragraphs to justify and support your view.

The same viewpoint should be stated in the conclusion.

If you feel there are two equal sides to the issue (for and against), you may decide to use an argument-led approach, (see Unit 8).

In thesis-led answers, you will be assessed on how well you present and support your opinions. In argument-led answers you must show that you can summarise and evaluate the argument logically, supporting both opinions with clear supporting evidence.

3 Writing the opening paragraph

A Read the exam question and the three introductions answering the question. Then answer the questions below.

> *The problems caused by work-related stress (such as loss of productivity) have become a concern for both employers and workers.*
>
> *What do you think are the main causes of work-related stress and how can they be avoided?*

A There are many problems caused by work-related stress, such as a loss of productivity, and this concerns employers and workers. Stress has many causes such as a heavy workload and time pressures. In this essay, I will discuss how workload and time pressures can cause stress, and I will offer some solutions to reduce them.

B Work-related stress has become a major cause for concern for both managers and employees since it has a negative effect on the health of workers. Consequently, productivity in the workplace suffers. In this essay, I will argue that unrealistic workloads and time pressures need to be addressed if we are to reduce stress levels.

C Time lost at work through stress and ill health is a cause for concern for both managers and employees. It can cause employees to miss work for long periods of time due to ill health and, naturally, this can cause problems for the company. No manager wants a worker who is often absent from work because of stress.

1 Which introduction does not present a clear opinion? ....
2 Which introduction has a clear opinion but uses the same words as the question? ....
3 Which introduction has a clear opinion and uses different words and phrases from the question? ....

B Now write your own introduction to answer the exam question in Section 2.

4 Presenting and justifying your opinion

The main paragraphs of an 'agree or disagree' essay should contain your presentation. Each point made in your presentation must be clearly justified with supporting material.

A The statements a–d below are all supporting material in answer to the exam question in 3A. Match them to the correct technique for justifying an opinion (1–4).

a Work-related stress is a problem because it undermines performance and is costly to employers. ....
b Research conducted by the government found that a large number of people in the UK experience .... work-related stress at a level they believe is affecting their health.
c The psychological effects of stress can be extreme. For instance, a work colleague of mine .... reported that he had suffered a nervous breakdown after a promotion had increased his workload to unmanageable proportions.
d If work-related stress is not dealt with, it could lead to extended employee absence, lower .... productivity and higher health care costs.

1 a statistic   **2** a scenario   **3** a reason   **4** an example

B For each of the statements below, practise justifying your opinion using a reason, a scenario or an example.

Work-related stress is a problem because ...

If work-related stress is not dealt with, ...

The psychological effects of stress can be extreme. For instance, ...

C Use one of the methods from Exercise 4A to justify your opinion on each of the following topics.

• Work should be the most important aspect of our lives.

• We work far too much these days.

• Children study too many useless subjects at school.

• Money is not the most important factor when choosing a career.

5 Expressing disagreement

Good writers often include a paragraph to refute (disagree with) the other side of the argument, even when using the thesis-led approach. This shows an ability to view the argument objectively before offering your own opinion.

A Look at the language in the box for refuting an argument.

> Critics may say ... . However ...
>
> It could be argued that ...
>
> It is difficult to accept this point of view as/because/since ...
>
> Although some people argue that ..., we should consider ...
>
> Despite claims that ..., it is a fact that ...
>
> While it might be argued that ..., the truth is ...
>
> Though it is true that ..., we should also bear in mind (that) ...

Expand on the following ideas with your own opinion, using language from the box.

1 Although people are paid to do a specific job, ...

2 While many people give their best at work, ...

3 Just because drama or music are not directly relevant to our future jobs, ...

4 To those who argue that automation is more reliable, ...

5 It might be argued that we work to earn money. However, ...

6 Despite the fact that there has been a reduction in scheduled working hours over the last three decades, ...

B Look at these opinions with a partner. Discuss the opposing points of view.

Studying performing arts subjects is a waste of time.

Women are too busy in the home to commit to full-time careers.

Now write one or two sentences to refute the statements using language from 5A above.

6 Writing the conclusion

The last paragraph of the essay forms your conclusion.

A Re-read the introductions in 3A. Then read the conclusions below and answer the questions.

1 In conclusion, because stress in the workplace causes such serious problems in terms of loss of company productivity and poor health for the employees, its causes need to be effectively addressed. By helping workers to manage workloads more efficiently and reducing time pressures placed on them, managers should be able to reduce the levels of stress experienced by their employees.

2 To sum up, work-related stress has become a major cause for concern both for managers and employees because it affects productivity. Managers need to reduce the workload of workers. It is also useful if training can be provided to assist workers in helping to deal with levels of stress.

- Which conclusion rephrases Introduction B on page 43 and summarises the main points? ....
- Which conclusion contains new information and doesn't paraphrase Introduction B on page 43? ....

B Now write your own conclusion for the essay question in 2A. Decide which approach to use.

7 Academic Writing Task 2: Essay

for this task

- ▶ Analyse the question and decide on your approach. If you choose a thesis-led approach, state your opinion in the introduction.

- ▶ Use the main paragraphs of your essay to present and develop your opinion. Make sure you justify each point with clear supporting material. Where appropriate, remember to refute the opposing opinion, providing a logical argument for doing so.

- ▶ Re-state your opinion succinctly in the conclusion in a different way from before.

You should spend about 40 minutes on this task.

Write about the following topic:

Most high-level positions in companies are filled by men even though the workforce in many developed countries is more than 50 per cent female. Companies should be required to allocate a certain percentage of these positions to women.

To what extent do you agree?

Give reasons for your answers and include any relevant examples from your own knowledge or experience.

Write at least 250 words.

Questions 1–4

Label the plan below.

Choose your answers from the box and write the letters **A–G** next to questions 1–4.

Vegetable Garden

A tall plants
B strawberries
C shed
D manure heap
E vegetable bed
F greenhouse
G compost bins

1 ...... *compost bins*
2 ...... *veg beds*
3 ...... *tall plants*
4 ...... *strawberries* *greenhouse*

Questions 5–7

Complete the flowchart below.

Write **NO MORE THAN THREE WORDS** for each answer.

Three-Year Crop Rotation Cycle

Year 1
Legumes (e.g. **5** *beans* ....) release nitrogen into soil.

↓

Year 2
Brassicas (e.g. cabbages and broccoli) have a **6** *high nitrogen requ...* ....

↓

Year 3
Potato family (e.g. tomatoes, peppers) have big leaves preventing the **7** ....

Questions 8–10

Label the diagram below.

*Write **NO MORE THAN THREE WORDS** for each answer.*

Compost Bin

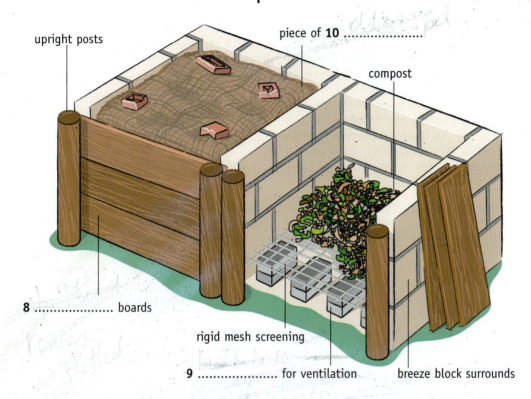

upright posts

piece of **10** ....

compost

8 .... boards

rigid mesh screening

9 .... for ventilation

breeze block surrounds

Uncovering the secrets of the Great Pyramid of Giza

1 For thousands of years, people have sought to unlock the secrets of the Great Pyramid. Constructed more than four millennia ago on the plains of Giza, near present-day Cairo, the Great Pyramid remains shrouded in mystery. Many theories have been proposed to explain its origin. Many believe it was simply a tomb or monument for an ancient pharaoh, others suggest it was an astronomical observatory, a huge sundial, or even a vast communication device to connect with other worlds.

2 The earliest existing description of the pyramids was written by the Greek historian Herodotus. After visiting Egypt in the fifth century BC, Herodotus described the four faces of the Great Pyramid as being covered with highly-polished limestone, with joints so fine that they were almost invisible. Four centuries later, the geographer Strabo wrote of a perfectly concealed, hinged stone located on the north face of the pyramid. The stone could be raised to form an entrance, but when closed was indistinguishable from the surrounding stone. The hidden entrance apparently gave access to a narrow passage that descended more than 350 feet into a damp, vermin-infested pit carved out of the bedrock directly beneath the base of the pyramid. However, by the 1st century AD, the whereabouts of this door had been lost.

3 In 820, Abdullah al-Ma'mun, the son of the Caliph of Baghdad, made the first major attempt to unlock the secrets of the Great Pyramid. After spending years fruitlessly searching for a secret entrance, al-Ma'mun finally ordered his team of workers to use battering rams to knock a hole directly through the pyramid's outer casing. The workmen then burrowed their way more than 100 feet into the core of the monument in the hope of finding a passage that would lead them to the pyramid's interior. With no passage in sight, the workmen were on the point of giving up, when they suddenly heard the sound of a falling rock to the east of the

tunnel. After digging their way toward the source of the noise, they emerged into a dark descending passageway.

4 Al-Ma'mun's fortunate discovery was a long, 3-foot wide passage that descended into the base of the pyramid at an angle of 26°. Working their way up the passageway, al-Ma'mun's workmen found the secret entrance to the pyramid that they had missed before, about 90 feet to the north and nearly 50 feet above the pyramid's base, much higher than al-Ma'mun had guessed. Further down the descending passage, the workers located the entrance to another ascending passageway which was blocked by three granite rocks. After cutting around the blocks, the workers climbed the passage until they came to the entrance of a high-roofed ascending corridor, known subsequently as the Grand Gallery. A low horizontal passage from the gallery's entrance led to an empty room now called the Queen's Chamber. At the top of the gallery, the workmen finally arrived at the King's Chamber with its five-storey vaulted ceiling. Despite searching everywhere for treasure, the only discovery was a large open coffin made of polished granite. The coffin lid – and the King's body – had long since been removed.

5 The first major study of the Great Pyramid was conducted in 1638 by John Greaves, an Oxford professor of astronomy and mathematics. Greaves noticed that near the lower entrance of the Grand Gallery was a narrow shaft, hidden in the wall, which had been dug straight down into the depths of the pyramid. This was the entrance to the so-called 'Well Shaft' which links the Grand Gallery with the descending passage. Using notches carved into the shaft's sides for support, Greaves was able to lower himself down to a small chamber about 60 feet beneath. The purpose of the shaft was a mystery to Greaves, although archaeologists have since suggested it was used as an exit route

for the Pharaoh's workers, once the granite blocks had been put in place.

6 In 1837, Colonel Howard Vyse, an English army officer, re-opened the original forced entryway that had been made by al-Ma'mun a thousand years earlier. Despite some destructive techniques (he used dynamite to blast his way through the pyramid), Vyse was able to make a number of significant discoveries, including air shafts leading from the King's Chamber to the outside of the pyramid which allow the chamber to remain at a constant 20°C. Vyse's greatest find, though, was a small piece of graffiti that gives the only clue to the pyramid's builder, the 4th Dynasty Pharaoh Khufu.

7 Research into the Great Pyramid took a new direction in 1864 when the Scottish astronomer Robert Menzies proposed that the monument is actually a chronological map of the world's history – past, present and future. According to Menzies, every inch of the pyramid represents one year, with major historical and biblical events represented by key locations within the pyramid's structure. Menzies also contended that the secret of this divinely-given storehouse of wisdom would remain sealed until a time when it would be most needed.

8 Inspired by Menzies and his followers, various other pyramidologists have proposed theories that attribute divine or alien guidance to the Great Pyramid's construction, despite the scepticism of the majority of archaeologists, engineers, and architects who instead attribute the pyramid's construction to human ingenuity. Today, the use of robotics and other advanced technology offers the prospect of being able to explore the pyramid's most remote spaces, making both groups of researchers hopeful that someday soon the Great Pyramid's secrets may finally be revealed.

Questions 1–5

Label the diagram below.

*Choose **NO MORE THAN THREE WORDS** from the reading passage for each answer.*

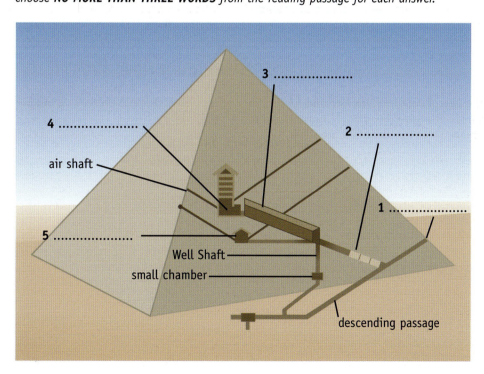

3 ....

4 ....

air shaft

2 ....

1 ....

5 ....

Well Shaft

small chamber

descending passage

Questions 6–10

Classify the following as relating to

A Abdullah al-Ma'mun
B John Greaves
C Colonel Howard Vyse
D Robert Menzies

*Write the correct letter **A**, **B**, **C** or **D** next to questions 6–10.*

6 discovered the name of the king who built the Great Pyramid.
7 found the interior passageways and chambers by a stroke of luck.
8 discovered an almost vertical, connecting passage.
9 discovered ventilation in parts of the interior.
10 claimed the pyramid holds as yet undisclosed truths which would become known in the future.

6 .....
7 .....
8 .....
9 .....
10 .....

Questions 11–13

Complete the notes below.

*Choose **NO MORE THAN THREE WORDS** from the passage for each answer.*

Ancient Descriptions of the Great Pyramid

• originally encased in **11** .... with an almost smooth surface
• entered by a hidden door on **12** .... of pyramid
• unpleasant underground room had **13** .... living in it

---

▶ WRITING TASK 2

You should spend about 40 minutes on this task.

Write about the following topic:

> *The problem with society today is that it is essentially unbalanced, with some people being paid huge salaries to work very long hours, whilst others do not have a job and have too much time on their hands. There is no middle ground.*
>
> *Do you agree or disagree?*

Give reasons for your answers and include any relevant examples from your knowledge or experience.

Write at least 250 words.

SPEAKING

PART 2
Example task
Read the topic card below carefully.
You will have to talk about the topic for one to two minutes.
You have one minute to think about what you are going to say.
You can make notes to help you if you wish.

> **Describe something successful you have done.**
> **You should say:**
>   **what you did**
>   **how you prepared for it**
>   **what kind of positive response you received**
> **and explain why it was important for you.**

PART 3
Example questions
• How would you define success?
• Do you think society places too much emphasis on money as a measurement of success?
• What do you think distinguishes successful people from unsuccessful ones?
• What makes some companies successful and other companies not?

Climate and the Environment

> **Exam tasks** ▸ Yes/No/Not given; sentence completion
> **Skills** ▸ Analysing meaning; identifying paraphrase

1 Introduction

A Look at the statements a–j. Do you agree or disagree? Tick (✔) the appropriate box.

GREEN-O-METER
How green R U?

	Agree	Disagree
a You should buy food produced locally.	☐	☐
b Taking holidays in a less developed country helps its economy.	☐	☐
c Cycle lanes are OK, but roads are vital for building the economy.	☐	☐
d If you buy wood, you should check it came from a sustainable source.	☐	☐
e Developing a poor country's economy is more important than saving its wildlife.	☐	☐
f Technology can solve all our environmental problems.	☐	☐
g You should only use your car if it's essential.	☐	☐
h You should buy food that is organic and comes in reusable packaging.	☐	☐
i When you leave a room, you should turn off the lights.	☐	☐
j Governments should use cleaner sources of energy.	☐	☐

B Compare your answers with a partner. Then discuss the following questions.

1 Why do you agree or disagree with each statement?

2 Which statements are about attitude and which are about actions?

3 In which statements are the opinions 'green'?

4 Do you do any of the 'green' actions mentioned? Why/Why not?

C Do you have any other ideas about how we should help protect the environment? Discuss with a partner.

IN THE EXAM

Reading module: Yes/No/Not given; sentence completion

In the Reading module, your understanding of the writer's ideas and attitudes may be tested. For Yes/No/Not given tasks, you are presented with a list of statements, which may or may not be the same as the message the writer presents in the text. You have to decide if the statement matches the writer's message or not.

In sentence completion tasks you are required to complete sentences so that they have the same meaning as information in the text. Depending on the task type, you might be asked to select words taken either directly from the text or from a list of options.

2 Analysing meaning

A Skim the following text to get an understanding of the main idea.

The Changing Ocean

SCIENTISTS have long stated that the main effect of global warming is the melting of the polar ice caps, resulting in a rise in sea levels. However, as we observe the theory become a reality, it is becoming apparent that this phenomenon also has multifarious secondary effects.

Fresh water from melting ice caps flows into the sea reducing the concentration of salt in the water and thus the sea's density. Saline-dense water would normally sink to the sea bed and then travel to warmer equatorial regions. Concurrently, the warmer, less densely saline water in warmer parts of the world would travel along the sea surface to the poles, where its salinity would increase and the water would consequently sink. However, as the salinity of polar water decreases, this ocean process slows down. This cycle is vital, however, as it has an oxygenating effect on the water and also carries nutrients from deeper water to the surface. Therefore, any slowing down of the cycle may have dramatic consequences for sea life.

A second alarming discovery is that the sea itself has traditionally played a role in reducing global warming. Oceans hold within them a certain amount of carbon dioxide. As the temperature of the sea rises, so its capacity to hold CO_2 falls, thus the problem of global warming is further exacerbated. However, there is a piece of good news to counter this: melting ice caps and lower saline levels enable the sea to hold more carbon dioxide, so the problem could be offset to some extent.

B Re-read the second paragraph carefully. Answer the questions below, following the thought processes.

For each question, answer
- ▸ **YES** if the statement expresses EXACTLY the same idea expressed in the passage.
- ▸ **NO** if the statement expresses an OPPOSITE idea from the one expressed in the passage.
- ▸ **NOT GIVEN** if the statement expresses an idea NOT MENTIONED in the passage.

1 Dense water travels more slowly than warmer surface water.
- ▸ Does the writer talk about water with a dense saline content?
- ▸ Does the writer also compare the speed of warm water and cold water?
- ▸ If you cannot answer 'Yes' to this second question, then the idea in the sentence is not mentioned by the writer and you should answer *NOT GIVEN*.

2 Nutrients are circulated less effectively as the salinity level of the sea in the polar regions decreases.
- ▸ Is the idea of nutrients mentioned in the text?
- ▸ If the answer is 'yes', does the writer express the same idea as in the sentence? i.e. lower saline levels will lead to nutrients not being circulated in the ocean.
- ▸ If the idea in the text is exactly the same as the sentence, you should answer *YES*.

3 More fresh water pouring into the sea accelerates the ocean cycle.
- ▸ Does the writer talk about an increase in fresh water entering the sea?
- ▸ If the answer is 'yes', does the writer talk about the ocean cycle getting faster (accelerating) or slowing down?
- ▸ If the ocean cycle is getting faster, the text expresses the same idea as the sentence and you should answer *YES*. If the ocean cycle is slowing down, the text expresses the opposite idea to the sentence, and you should answer *NO*.

C Now do the same for these questions about the third paragraph, following a similar thought process.
1 Rising sea temperatures are mainly due to the sea being less able to hold carbon dioxide.
2 Rising sea temperatures have resulted in the sea becoming less effective in curbing global warming.
3 Seas with higher fresh water content retain more carbon dioxide.

3 Identifying paraphrase

A With a partner, look at the title of the following text. What environmental problem do you think the text discusses?

B Skim the text to see if your predictions were correct.

C Reading module questions often require you to identify synonyms and paraphrase. Match the following words from the text to their synonyms.

1 encourage
2 make it clear
3 inhale
4 fossil
5 boost

a carbon-based
b breathe in
c provide a new impetus
d send out a message
e promote

Environmental enemy No. 1

The Cost of Coal

1 IS ECONOMIC GROWTH bad for the environment? It is certainly fashionable in some quarters to argue that trade and capitalism are choking the planet to death. Yet, there is little evidence to back up such alarmism. On the contrary, there is reason to believe not only that growth can be compatible with environmentalism, but that it often bolsters it.

2 This is not, however, to say that there aren't any environmental problems to worry about. In particular, the needlessly unhealthy and inefficient way in which we use energy is the biggest source of environmental fouling. That is why it makes sense to start a slow shift away from today's filthy use of fossil fuels towards a cleaner, low-carbon future. There are three reasons for calling for such an energy revolution.

3 First, a switch to cleaner energy would make tackling other green concerns a lot easier. That is because dealing with many of these energy concerns, e.g. treating chemical waste, recycling aluminium or burning rubbish, is an energy-intensive task.

4 The second reason is that burning fossil fuels is having a massive effect on climate change. The most sensible way for governments to tackle this problem is to send a powerful signal that the

world must move towards a low-carbon future. That would spur all sorts of innovations in clean energy.

5 The third reason is the most pressing of all: human health. In poor countries, where inefficient power stations, sooty coal boilers and bad ventilation are the norm, air pollution is one of the leading but preventable causes of death. It affects the rich world, too: from Athens to Beijing, multitudes are affected by the inhalation of fine carbon particles released by the combustion of fossil fuels.

Dethroning King Coal

6 The dream of cleaner energy will never be realised as long as the balance tips towards dirty technology. For a start, governments must stop subsidies and exemptions that actually encourage the consumption of fossil fuels.

7 Some of these subsidies, such as cash given to the coal industry, are blatantly foolhardy. Others are less obvious, but

no less damaging. There are currently coal plants using technology over 30 years old, yet they are exempt from the legislation which aims to reduce the harmful emissions they produce. Far from trying to close these plants down, in some cases certain measures have been announced giving these production facilities a new lease of life. This blame can be laid at the door of rich and poor countries alike; many developing countries subsidise electricity heavily in the name of helping poor people, but rich farmers and urban elites guzzle the largest share of cheap, fossil power.

8 A second recommendation is for the rich world to help poorer countries switch to cleaner energy. The International Energy Agency has estimated that there are 1.6 billion people in the world who are unable to use modern energy. They often walk many miles to fetch wood, or collect cow dung to use as fuel. As the poor world grows richer in the coming decades and builds thousands of power plants, many of these people will get electricity. However, many of these plants will burn coal in a dirty way. The rich world must be ready to pay for the poor to change to low-carbon energy. This should not be regarded as charity, but rather as a form of insurance against global warming.

9 The final and most crucial step is to start pricing energy properly. At the moment, the harm done to human health and the environment from burning fossil fuels is not reflected in the price of non-renewable fuels in most countries. There is no perfect way to do this, but one good idea is for governments to impose a tax based on carbon emissions. Such a tax could be introduced gradually, with the revenues raised returned as reductions in, say, labour tax. That would make it absolutely clear that the time has come to stop burning dirty fuels such as coal.

The dawning of the age of hydrogen

10 None of these changes kill off coal altogether. Rather, they would provide a much-needed boost to the development of low-carbon technologies. Naturally, renewable energy such as solar and wind power will get a boost. But so too would 'sequestration', an innovative way of using fossil fuels without releasing carbon into the air.

11 This is important for two reasons. For a start, there is so much cheap coal, distributed all over the world, that poor countries are bound to burn it. The second reason is that sequestration offers a fine stepping-stone to squeaky-clean hydrogen energy. Once the energy trapped in coal is unleashed and its carbon sequestered, energy-laden hydrogen can be used directly in fuel cells. These nifty inventions can power a laptop, car or home without any harmful emissions at all.

12 It will take time to establish this hydrogen age, but there are promising signs. Within a few years, nearly every big car manufacturer plans to have fuel-cell cars on the road. Power plants using this technology are already trickling onto the market. Most big oil companies have active hydrogen and carbon-sequestration efforts under way. Even some green groups opposed to all fossil-fuel burning say they are willing to accept sequestration as a bridge to a renewable-based hydrogen future. But best of all, this approach offers even the staunchest defenders of coal a realistic long-term plan for tackling climate change.

Source: The Economist

4 Yes/No/Not Given

for this task

In the IELTS exam, your understanding of the writer's ideas and attitudes is tested. You are presented with a list of statements, which may or may not be the same as the message the writer presents in the text. You have to decide if the statement matches the writer's message or not. The questions appear in the same order as the information presented in the text.

▶ To locate the information in the text, pick out the keywords in the statement, then find the information in the text by looking for synonyms and paraphrase.

▶ Use the order of the questions as a 'map'. Locate the right part of the text quickly, then spend more time choosing the correct answer.

▶ Answer *Yes*, if the statement means the same as the message in the text.

▶ Answer *No*, if the statement contradicts (says the opposite of) the message in the text.

▶ Answer *Not given*, if the statement says something not mentioned in the text. The question may relate very closely to an idea expressed by the writer but not have EXACTLY the same idea. In this case you would answer *Not given*. For this reason you should read very carefully to decide precisely what the writer is saying.

Questions 1–7

Do the following statements agree with the views of the writer in the passage?

Answer

YES　　　*if the statement agrees with the views of the writer*
NO　　　*if the statement contradicts the views of the writer*
NOT GIVEN　*if it is impossible to say what the writer thinks about this*

express tip

Don't answer *Yes* because you think it is true – what does it say in the text?

1 Deaths resulting from carbon-based air pollution occur mainly in the developing world. *Yes*
2 Developed countries are mainly to blame for promoting the coal industry. *No*
3 The world's energy requirements are set to increase dramatically in the future. *Not given*
4 Switching to non-carbon fuels will have the added benefit of stimulating economic growth in poorer countries. *Not given*
5 Developed countries have a moral responsibility to help developing countries change to low-carbon energy. *No*
6 A tax on carbon emissions could be used to fund the building of cleaner power plants. *Yes No*
7 The technology behind sequestration was first developed by major oil production companies. *not given*

5 Sentence completion

for this task

There are two types of sentence completion tasks. In the first type you are given sentences which you have to complete using words taken directly from the text.

▸ Look for keywords and paraphrase in the sentence to help you locate the correct part of the text.

▸ Use exactly the same words as in the text – do not paraphrase or change them in any way. If you change the words, your answer will be incorrect.

▸ Check the maximum number of words you can use. A hyphenated word such as 'long-term' counts as one word.

In the second type of sentence completion task, you are asked to complete sentences from a list of options. The completed sentence will have the same meaning as the information in the text.

▸ Quickly locate the relevant section of the text and re-read carefully. The questions may focus on information in one part of the text or they may be spread throughout the text, but they will always be in the same order as the text.

▸ There are extra options that you will not need.

▸ The first answer you choose may not be correct; often more than one option will relate to the information required but only one option will match EXACTLY the idea stated in the text. Match the ones you are sure about first, and go back to the others at the end of the task.

▸ Make sure the completed sentence has the same meaning as the text AND is grammatically correct.

Questions 8–12

Complete the sentences below with words taken from the reading passage.
Use **NO MORE THAN THREE WORDS** for each answer.

8 The burning of carbon-based ....*air pollution*.... releases carbon into the air. ✗   *fossil fuels*

9 Polluted air is one of the world's major ......*problem*...... ✗ ... *Causes of death*

10 Governments should ..*tax based*.... ✗ ... on carbon emissions in order to price energy sensibly.   '*impos tax*

11 Rather than halting the burning of coal altogether, ...*naturally*........ would be given a new impetus such as renewables and sequestration.   *low carbon* ✗

12 Vehicle manufacturers intend to produce ......*fuel cell*.... in the near future.   *mannfactue* ✗   *cars*

Questions 13–16

Complete each sentence with the correct ending **A–H** from the box below.

express tip

As all the questions are in the same order as the information in the text, you can use the questions as a 'map' to help you find your way around the text.

13 Government cash subsidies given to the coal industry .... E

14 The poor world continuing to get richer .... ✗ F

15 A sensible government energy pricing policy *6-9* ......H

16 The process of sequestration *10–11* ......A....

> **A** produces clean power from burning fossil fuels.
>
> **B** encourages an improvement in environmental conditions.
>
> **C** causes health problems in the developing world.
>
> **D** is essential for the reprocessing of waste materials.
>
> **E** promotes the burning of carbon fuels.
>
> **F** means more and more dirty energy will be generated in the future.
>
> **G** has led to an increase in the use of renewable energy.
>
> **H** would send out a message that dirty energy production must be stopped.

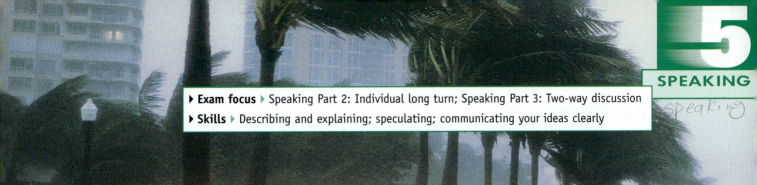

> **Exam focus** ▸ Speaking Part 2: Individual long turn; Speaking Part 3: Two-way discussion
> **Skills** ▸ Describing and explaining; speculating; communicating your ideas clearly

1 Introduction

Discuss these questions with a partner.
• How will climate change have altered the world in 100 years?
• Do you think the future of climate change is in the hands of governments or individuals?

2 Describing and explaining

In Part 2 of the Speaking module, you are asked to speak for 1–2 minutes about a topic. Part 2 tests two speaking functions: describing and explaining. You will be expected to demonstrate a command of each function.

Look at the topic card below.

> **Describe an experience when the weather was either very hot or very cold.**
> **You should say:**
> > **when it was**
> > **what you did**
> > **what clothes you wore**
> **and explain why you like or dislike this type of weather.**

🎧 **A** **5.1** Listen to the final part of two candidates' responses to the topic card. Make notes on what you heard, then compare with a partner.

🎧 **B** **5.2** What phrases did each speaker use to introduce their explanation? Listen again.

C Tell your partner which kind of weather you prefer and why. Use the language in the box below to introduce your explanation.

> The reason why (I don't like) ... is that ...   One of the reasons is that ...
> One of the things ... about ... is ...   What I like/dislike ... is ...

IN THE EXAM

Speaking Module Part 2: Individual long turn

The examiner will give you a card with some instructions. You will be asked to follow the instructions and talk about a particular topic, drawing on your own personal experience. You will have one minute preparation time in which you should make notes to help you organise your ideas and aid you in speaking about the various points on the card.

The examiner will not speak until the end of this part of the exam, when he or she will ask you one or two brief questions to round off your talk. This part of the module lasts about 3–4 minutes, including the one minute's preparation time.

SPEAKING

3 Speculating

In Part 3 you may be asked to compare and contrast two things, or to speculate on a hypothetical situation related to the topic you discussed in Part 2.

A Look at the following questions. Which question asks you to compare and contrast and which asks you to speculate?

    1 Do you think governments will make climate change a higher priority in the future?

    2 If you want to encourage people to use public transport, is it better to make buses and trains cheaper or place a higher tax on cars and fuel?

 B **5.3** Listen to two candidates answering Question 1. Which answer is better? Why?

 C **5.4** Listen again to the better response. What language does the speaker use to speculate?

D Look again at the language used for speculating.

<table>
<tr><td>might/may/could</td><td>probably/probably not</td></tr>
<tr><td>It's (very) likely/unlikely that ... will</td><td>will definitely/probably definitely/probably won't</td></tr>
</table>

> **express tip**
>
> Listen carefully to what type of question the examiner is asking you. Be prepared to respond using the appropriate language.

Discuss the following questions with a partner. Use language from the box in your answers.

a How will climate change affect where people live in a hundred years?

b Will we recycle all our waste in a hundred years?

c How will we solve environmental problems in the future?

4 Communicating your ideas clearly

A Whether you are introducing an idea, explaining, or offering an example, it is a good idea to use signpost words and phrases to indicate what you are going to say before you say it. Look at the following sentence.

We are beginning to see the effects of global warming, for instance, we have started to see sea levels rising.

'For instance' tells the listener that they are going to hear an example.

Now look at the following sentence beginning and discuss with a partner how it might continue.

There is much we can do to help reduce global warming, for instance ...

 B **5.5** Listen to four candidates answering some more Part 3 questions on global warming. Each candidate uses signpost words to help the listener follow their ideas.

Complete the table with the signpost words that the speakers use.

Speaker	Signpost word function	Signpost words
1	setting out an outline of your response	1 There are two main problems: firstly ... In addition to this ...
2	introducing an example	2 ....
3	introducing a result or consequence	3 ....
4	introducing a reason or cause	4 ....

C Look at the Part 3 question below and the four responses which follow. In pairs, complete each response with your own ideas, remembering to use suitable signpost words. Then role-play the answers.

> What can we do as individuals to help save the environment?
> ▸ Governments are finally listening to the public on green issues …
> ▸ There are two things we can do …
> ▸ Many people in my city have started to leave their car at home and cycle to work …
> ▸ There are lots of simple things we can do to save energy around the home …

5 Individual long turn

for this task

▸ Make notes to help you talk about the card – include any keywords and high-level vocabulary you want to use.

▸ Highlight any keywords on the card.

▸ Introduce your reasons using appropriate language and take the opportunity to demonstrate your speaking skills.

Work in pairs. Practise the interview.

Student A: You are the candidate. For one minute, look at the topic card below and make notes. Then, use your notes to speak for one or two minutes. Follow the advice in the *for this task* box.

Student B: You are the examiner. Give Student A one minute to prepare. Then listen to Student A's answers carefully. Did Student A follow the advice in the *for this task* box? After one or two minutes, interrupt and ask a few questions relating to the topic. When you have finished, change roles.

> **Describe something you do which is environmentally friendly.**
> **You should say:**
> **what you do**
> **when you do it**
> **if you find it easy or difficult**
> **and explain why you think this activity is important.**

6 Two-way discussion

for this task

▸ Give full answers to each question.

▸ Look out for questions which give you the chance to speculate about the topic. Use appropriate language to speculate such as 'may' or 'it's unlikely'.

▸ Organise your ideas mentally before you begin speaking.

▸ Communicate your ideas clearly by using appropriate signpost words.

Work in pairs. Practise the two-way discussion.

Student A: You are the candidate. Listen to the questions and answer as fully as possible. Don't forget to express and justify your opinions. Do the questions require you to speculate?

Student B: You are the examiner. Use the questions below and interview Student A for 4–5 minutes. Listen to Student A's answers carefully. Does he or she express and justify opinions given? Does he or she speculate about the future? What language is used to speculate? When you have finished, change roles.

- How will we produce energy in the future?
- How have people's attitudes to the environment changed in your country?
- Do people recycle household waste in your country?
- How will we travel around in the future?

express tip
You might be asked a closed question, where it is possible to simply answer *Yes/No*. It is very important to expand on your answer and provide more information to gain extra marks.

6 Globalisation

▶ **Exam tasks** ▶ Classification; sentence completion; notes completion
▶ **Exam focus** ▶ Listening Section 3: Academic dialogue
▶ **Skills** ▶ Listening and writing simultaneously; identifying distractors; understanding meaning

1 Introduction

A Discuss these questions in small groups.

- What is 'globalisation'? What areas of life are affected by globalisation? Give examples.
- Do you know any multinational companies or organisations? Why do you think they became globalised?

B Below are some consequences of globalisation. In a group, discuss whether they are positive or negative.

- Increased international trade
- Increase in exchange of ideas
- Emergence of a global language
- Rising influence of multinational companies
- Switching of production to countries with low labour costs

2 Listening and writing simultaneously

In the Listening module the answers often come quite close together, so you have to be able to write the answer to one question while listening for the answer to the next.

Look at the notes below for a reading assignment.

Reading assignment

Title: **1** The ...., the Future Is Global
Author: **2** ....
Publisher: **3** ....
Year published: **4** ....
Must get **5** .... edition

IN THE EXAM

Listening Section 3: Academic dialogue

Section 3 is an academic dialogue. It features a discussion between two or three people, usually students or students and a tutor. The questions may relate to opinion rather than fact. Notes and sentence completion tasks are common in this exam section, as well as classification questions.

Classification questions require you to select the answers to a range of questions from a short list of possible answers. There is only one answer to each question, but you may use each answer more than once.

A `6.1` Listen to the first part of the recording and identify the answer to Question 1. Do not write the answer yet.

B `6.2` Now listen to the next part of the recording. As you do so, write the answer to Question 1 and identify the answer to Question 2.

C `6.3` Now listen to the rest of the recording, listening and writing simultaneously. Write the answer to Question 2 while you are listening for the answer to Question 3, etc.

3 Identifying distractors

A With some task types, it helps to identify exactly what question is being asked. Look at this example from a sentence completion task. When completing the gap in the sentence, what question are you effectively answering? What are the keywords in the question? Can you predict the answer?

> **1** Alison thinks WTO rules do not favour *Companies* from wealthy countries.
>
> *smaller*

B `6.4` Now listen to the first part of the conversation and answer the question.

C Look at this extract from the conversation you have just heard.

> **Alison:** What do you mean, Dave?
> **Dave:** WTO rules favour the larger companies from wealthy countries.
> **Alison:** In what way?
> **Dave:** Well, by prohibiting protection through discriminatory tariffs, it's hard for poor countries to build up domestic industries.
> **Alison:** That may be the case, but I'm sure that's not a deliberate policy. Anyway you could argue that the rules laid down by the World Trade Organisation don't exactly help smaller companies from the richer nations either.

- What distracting information is in this extract? Identify and cross out any distractors.
- Identify and circle the correct answer.
- Which words prepared you for the correct answer? Underline the words that led you to the answer.

D `6.5` Listen to the rest of the conversation and answer Questions 2 and 3.

> **2** Dave believes the WTO *weakens* democracy throughout the world.
> **3** Alison thinks the WTO should regulate *Seed Companies.*

E Now turn to page 124 and read listening script 6.5. Repeat the steps for Questions 2 and 3.

4 Understanding meaning

In the Listening module, answers are usually stated *explicitly*. However, in tasks such as classification, the answer may be *implied* or expressed in an indirect way. Attitude may be expressed more clearly through intonation than through words.

6 6

A **6.6** Listen to the recording. Are the statements below true or false? Circle the answer.

1 The British will probably sign the contract.	**T**/ F
2 The French would never agree to such a deal.	T /**F**
3 The offer will probably be improved.	T /**F**
4 The two speakers disagree with each other.	T /**F**
5 This is bad news.	T /**F**
6 This is good news.	T /**F**

In what ways do the speakers in situations 1–4 express their opinion? How is meaning expressed in Questions 5 and 6?

B Look at the classification task below. Classification tasks expect you to 'read between the lines' and analyse the speaker's attitude and opinion.

disagree

express tip

Watch out for those distractors! The correct answer can often come after the distractor.

> **Questions 1–5**
> *Who thinks the following?*
>
> The Internet
>
> **A** Katya
> **B** Peter
> **C** both Katya and Peter
>
> 1 has aided globalisation. *A* .....C.
> 2 has helped people in some developing countries. *A* .....A.
> 3 is not too commercial. .....B.
> 4 creates new gaps between rich and poor. .....A.
> 5 is a form of cultural imperialism. *A* .....A.
>
> *Write the correct letter **A**, **B** or **C** next to questions 1–5.*

6.7 Look at Question 1 above. Listen to the first part of the recording and answer these questions.
- Does Peter think the Internet has aided globalisation? What are his exact words?
- Does Katya agree with him? How does she express her opinion?
- Which is the correct answer, **A**, **B** or **C**?

C **6.8** Now listen carefully to the rest of the recording and answer Questions 2–5.

5 Classification

for this task

Before you listen	▶ Make sure your answer is actually the answer you need and not a distractor.
▶ Identify keywords in the question. Can you think of any synonyms or paraphrases?	
As you listen	▶ You do not have to write the full answer, just use the code provided.
▶ Listen for the keywords and any synonyms.	

 6.9 *Questions 1–4*

What do the students say about the following books?

A 'Hands off the Planet' by Ted Crilly
B 'The Future Is Bright, The Future Is Global' by Dr Jack Jones
C both books

Write the correct letter **A**, **B** or **C** next to questions 1–4.

1 easily available .....A.

2 difficult to follow ~~A~~ .....B.

3 unsuitable for newcomers to the subject .....B.

4 could be better organised .....B.

6 Sentence completion and notes completion

for this task

Notes and sentence completion	**As you listen**
Notes completion questions have to be completed using words from the recording.	▶ Make sure that your answer is actually the answer you need and not a distractor.
Sentence completion questions are similar, but you should ensure your answer is grammatically correct.	▶ Keep listening – the answers can come quite close together.
Before you listen	**After you listen**
▶ Check how many words you can use.	Make sure you have not exceeded the word limit and check your spelling.
▶ Identify the question, answer type and keywords.	
▶ Can you think of any synonyms for the keywords? Can you predict the answer?	

6.10 *Questions 5–8*

Complete the sentences below.

*Write **NO MORE THAN THREE WORDS** for each answer.*

express tip

Listen carefully to make sure you understand the speakers' opinions.

5 Brad thinks that Crilly's section on the globalisation of the media was .....well....research. ✓

6 Janet feels that Crilly tends to ignore any facts that do not .....support....his argument.

7 Janet thinks that 'Hands off the Planet' is insufficiently .....academic.... to be taken seriously.

8 Brad thinks the .....bibliography.... in 'Hands off the Planet' could be improved.

6.11 *Questions 9–12*

Complete the notes below.

*Write **NO MORE THAN THREE WORDS** for each answer.*

express tip

Be alert. Keep listening for those keywords, even when you are writing.

Business studies writing assignment

Title: Globalisation: **9** .....Right or wrong.....

Number of words **10** .....1500.....

Submission date: **11** .....28 Feb 2.....

Send by **12** .....post.....

Ri to rong

internal

6 WRITING

> ▶ **Exam task** ▶ Describing charts and graphs
> ▶ **Exam focus** ▶ Academic Writing Task 1
> ▶ **Skills** ▶ Describing trends; describing a process

1 Introduction

Look at the pictures and discuss these questions with a partner.

- Apart from making calls, what can mobile phones be used for? If you have a mobile phone, what do you use it for?
- Which countries produce mobile phones? Where was your phone manufactured, and where did you buy it?

2 Describing trends

A Look at the first graph on the opposite page. What does it show? Discuss these questions with a partner.

1 What do the numbers on the vertical axis represent?
2 What time frame is shown on the horizontal axis and in the title?
3 What tense would you use if you were writing about this information? Why?
4 Where are the important peaks, troughs or changes in this period? Highlight them.
5 How does the March 2005 price differ from the March 2004 price?
6 What was the general trend from March 2004 to August 2004?
7 What was the general trend from August 2004 to March 2005?
8 How would you divide the information into stages?

IN THE EXAM

Academic writing module: Task 1

In Task 1 you are required to report information; you should not speculate or offer an opinion that is outside the given data.

You may be given a diagram (e.g. bar chart, pie chart or line graph), or a table. You are required to present the data using your own words. You should start by providing a clear introductory statement and then focus on key trends in the main paragraphs. Highlight key details, mentioning actual figures, then finish with a short summary.

In Task 1 you may instead be asked to report on a process, though this type is less common. Decide where the cycle begins/ends, if applicable, and make sure you cover all the stages shown in the diagram.

B Complete the sentences with information from the graph above and phrases from the Language Bank at the back of the book.

1 In April 2004 there was ....

2 Nokia share prices .... in the period shown.

3 Between May and July ....

4 From September to December ....

C Look at the graph below and answer 1–5 and 8 from 2A for this graph.

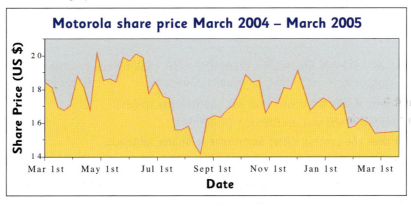

D Now complete the description below using phrases from the Language Bank at the back of the book.

The graph shows the changes and **1** .... overall in the share price of Motorola in a one-year period from March 2004 to March 2005.

At the beginning of this period the share price was at $17 per share. There were **2** .... until around mid-April when there was a **3** .... from $16.50 to $20.50. This higher price did not last long, however, and it fell before rising slightly again by June. From mid-June there was a **4** .... until mid-August when it **5** .... in this period at just over $14 per share. After that the share price recovered and, despite some fluctuations, continued to **6** .... until it **7** .... of $19 in December. Until March 2005 the trend was **8** .... again, ending the year at just over $15.

Motorola made significant gains and losses during this period but overall lost around $2 per share.

E Now write a similar description of the graph at the top of this page using your answers from 2A and language from the Language Bank at the back of the book. Remember to add specific figures and data to support your points.

3 Describing a process

A Look at the Task 1 question below and answer the questions.

The diagram below shows the stages a company should go through before launching a product globally.

Summarise the information by selecting and reporting the main features, and make comparisons where relevant.

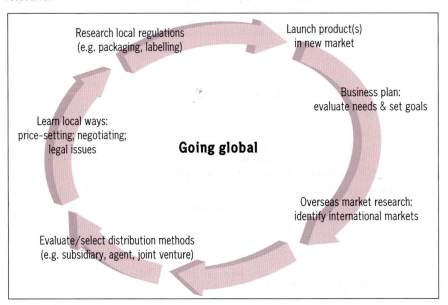

1 Where do you think this process starts and ends? Look for clues in the title and prompts. Is there a clear beginning?

2 How many stages are there? How will you link the stages?

3 What tense(s) will you use? Why?

4 What does the process show? Summarise it in one sentence.

B Complete the summary below using words from the box. Not all the words are needed.

Time	Order	Reason	Example
after that	first	so that	such as
once/when/after	next	in order to	for example
as soon as	finally		for instance

The diagram shows the six main stages that a company should follow when launching a product internationally in a new market.

1 .... go global with a product, the 2 .... thing you need to do is prepare an international business plan which will help you evaluate your needs and set goals for your company. 3 .... extensive market research needs **to be conducted** overseas. This will help you identify the potential international markets for your particular product.

4 .... it is important to evaluate and select the right methods of distribution for your product abroad. There are several ways to do this, 5 .... through company-owned foreign subsidiaries, by working through agents, or by setting up joint ventures. 6 .... you have

chosen the distribution method, familiarise yourself with local methods of setting prices and negotiating deals. It is also a good idea to find out what legal matters **are involved** in exporting so that you don't make any mistakes.

Before your product **can be launched** in the new market, make sure you comply with local regulations:
7 .... in your packaging and labelling. Following these six stages should ensure success in the new market.

Look at the phrases in the description in bold. What is this structure called? When and why is it used?

4 Academic Writing Task 1: Report

for this task

▸ Decide a starting point on the diagram to begin your report. In your introductory statement sum up what the diagram represents and state how many stages there are.

▸ Which tenses are appropriate? Do the prompts contain verbs? Decide if the verbs given need to be active or passive voice. Select the appropriate language you will use to connect ideas and stages.

▸ Paraphrase the information in the diagram where possible, but take care that it retains the same meaning as the information given.

▸ Remember to use a minimum of 150 words and don't spend more than twenty minutes on this section.

EXAM PRACTICE

You should spend about 20 minutes on this task.

The diagram shows how a transaction works from an ATM (automated teller machine).

Summarise the information by selecting and reporting the main features, and make comparisons where relevant.

Write at least 150 words.

express tip

The passive voice is useful in this task type. Decide if it would be appropriate to use the passive voice for some of the sentences, but make sure you use a variety of structures overall.

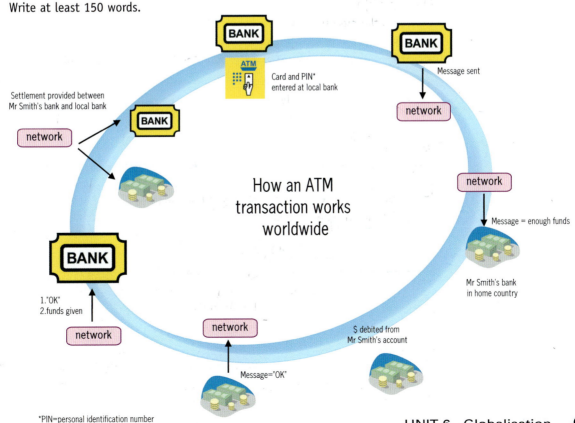

*PIN=personal identification number

Questions 1–3

Complete the notes below.

Write **NO MORE THAN TWO WORDS AND/OR A NUMBER** for each answer.

Reasons for Decline in UK Bird Population
Changes in methods of farming

- Increased use of **1** ....
- Changes in **2** .... times
- Drainage and ploughing of **3** ....
- Removal and neglect of hedgerows

Questions 4–6

Which species of bird appears on each conservation category list?

Choose your answers from the box and write the letters **A–F** next to the questions 4–6.

> **A** Blackbird
> **B** Canada Goose
> **C** Lapwing
> **D** Parrot
> **E** Skylark
> **F** Swift

4 red list: ....
5 amber list: ....
6 green list: ....

Questions 7–10

Complete the sentences below.

Write **NO MORE THAN THREE WORDS AND/OR A NUMBER** *for each answer.*

7 The RSPB aims to halt the .... by lobbying the government.

8 Only those farmers who use environmentally friendly methods would receive
   ....

9 By turning off seed drills for just a few seconds, small .... areas would be
   created.

10 If these areas were made on only .... of arable land, the skylark could be
   saved.

The shape of buildings to come

From the outside it's as sleek as a rocket, but is the Swiss Re tower really as sensational as it looks? Jonathan Glancey finds out.

1 It already has a nickname: a dumb one – the Gherkin. I am not sure where this name originated, but it is hopelessly inappropriate, even if it's likely to stick. Gherkins do not look like this. Nor is 30 St Mary Axe, in any accepted understanding of the word, 'organic'. If it resembles anything, it is one of the great dirigibles* of the 1930s, or Wernher von Braun's early space rocket. Tethered firmly to the ground, this sleek and sensational machine for making money, this 'towering innuendo', commissioned and owned by financial services group Swiss Re, is home to around 4,000 workers. It is certainly a striking design, but does 30 St Mary Axe offer better conditions than workers have been used to? Is it more than yet another filing cabinet in the sky?

2 Client and architect have made great claims for the building's environmental efficiency. One of the less measurable ways in which the tower could be considered environmentally friendly is the manner in which, close up, it appears to be much smaller, or at least, much lower, than it is. In fact, it appears no higher than GMW's Commercial Union building (which is some 70m shorter), an illusion created by the fact that the top of the building is invisible from the square below.

3 Not only does the building's circular form make it appear much less bulky than it is, it channels considerably less wind at street level than many right-angled towers. This has been proven in wind-tunnel tests on a model of the building. The circular form also offers a generous public plaza at the base, while an arcade around the tower promises a number of up-coming shops.

4 The real environmental achievement here, however, is the internal design. What you see from the plaza and, in fact, from all corners of London, is a great sheath of steel, aluminium and glass. This is the building's skin. Just behind this is the great steel structure of the building, hidden on dull days, clearly visible when the sun shines. This structure, devised by the engineers, Arup, is a diagonal cage very much like the skeleton of Barnes Wallis's Second World War bombers. Intriguingly, this structure compresses during the day as the building loads up with people and stretches in the evening as it empties.

5 Spiralling up through the internal structure is a sequence of atriums. They are interrupted every six floors so that the updraft of air through the building does not become too strong. These atriums achieve many things: they let light deep into the building and allow diagonal views up and down through the building. But the main advantage is that their corkscrew shape creates different air pressures, ensuring that fresh air is sucked up through the building as well as through the office floors.

6 In addition, the windows on the skin of the building can be opened in mild weather to allow air to flow in and out. Roller blinds set between the steel skeleton and glass skin control glare and reduce heat. Heating, lighting and air-conditioning bills will be low

*a 'dirigible' is an airship

compared with most towers and, with daylight reaching desks at the core of the building, workers should feel well off.

7 The luckiest are able to reach the nose cone of the tower, where a restaurant and bar satisfies anyone with a craving for James Bond glamour. The bar, reached by a spiral staircase or glass lift from the 70-seat restaurant, looks very much like a Ken Adam film set: the lair of a villain with designs to take over the world. It is quite breathtaking. Sadly, it and its master-of-the-universe views are reserved for Swiss Re employees and their guests only.

This is a fine skyscraper and one of the shapes of things to come in the design of city-centre offices. However, it is not perfect: the building is, perhaps, a little too smooth for its own good. Detail is not so much pared down as polished away, as if the architects had tried to make it as sheer as an airship, without the touches that delight hand and eye. Its entrance is also problematic; carving an appropriate doorway into the base of this office rocket was always going to be difficult,

and the result seems a little crude, as if someone had opened up a cavity with a giant tin-opener and then tried a little too hastily to cover up their handiwork. It would, perhaps, have been better to have created more than one underground entrance, which might have swept those working here from the edges of the plaza up into the aluminium-lined entrance lobby, leaving the skin of the building unbroken. This a trick Oscar Niemeyer performed neatly and dramatically with the entrance of his 'crown-of-thorns' cathedral in Brasilia. Doubtless there are practical, not to mention security reasons why this could not have been.

8 The result is a fascinating building that undoubtedly raises the standard of city-centre office design, but one that should be regarded as a kind of work-in-progress: a marker on the way to a more responsible and attractive form of skyscraper. In a Britain of largely cynical, fast-buck, skin-deep, government-approved new architecture, this is one new building – not a gherkin – that deserves to be relished.

Source: *Guardian Unlimited*

Questions 1–6

Do the following statements agree with the views of the writer in the reading passage?

You should write

YES	*if the statement agrees with the views of the writer*
NO	*if the statement contradicts the views of the writer*
NOT GIVEN	*if it is impossible to say what the writer thinks about this*

1 The tower is sympathetic to the buildings around it. *Yes*
2 The interior spiral structure allows workers to move around the building easily. *Not given*
3 The tower provides a light and airy space for employees to work. *yes*
4 Running costs are relatively inexpensive. *Yes.*
5 The top of the tower provides spectacular views for the public. *NO.*
6 The exterior glass shell lacks detail. *yes.*

Questions 7–10

Complete each sentence with the correct ending **A–H** from the box below.

7 When you stand very near to the building, F
8 Due to the building's roundness, A
9 As the building fills with workers, G
10 As a result of the design of the spiral structure, C

around the building (handwritten)

A there is less wind produced at the base.
B it is a building Londoners should be proud of.
C the building is naturally ventilated.
D the tower offers a good view of the city.
E the stairs get very crowded at certain times of the day.
F it appears to be lower than it actually is.
G the structure is compacted by the extra weight.
H it offers a vision of the future.

Questions 11–14

Complete the sentences below with words taken from the reading passage.

Use **NO MORE THAN THREE WORDS** for each answer.

Write your answers next to 11–14.

- The building looks less a gherkin and more like a(n) **11** _dirigibles_
- The temperature and light levels can be regulated by closing **12** _Roller blinds_ or opening **13** _windows_.
- An additional **14** _underground_ would have left the exterior shell unspoilt.

▶ WRITING TASK 1

You should spend about 20 minutes on this task.

The graph below shows the total number of people travelling within the London area over a typical 24-hour period using three forms of transport (car, bus and underground).

Summarise the information by selecting and reporting the main features, and make comparisons where relevant.

Write at least 150 words.

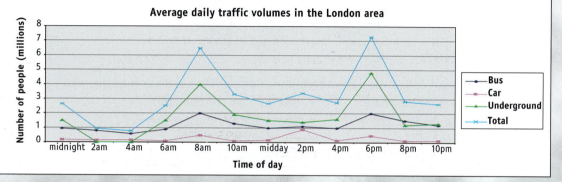

SPEAKING

PART 2
Example task
Read the topic card below carefully.
You will have to talk about the topic for one to two minutes.
You have one minute to think about what you are going to say.
You can make notes to help you if you wish.

> **Describe a film that you have seen recently.**
> **You should say:**
>   **who you saw the film with**
>   **who the main characters in the film are**
>   **what happens in the film**
> **and explain why you would recommend it or not.**

PART 3
Example questions
• Do you think it's best to see foreign films in their original language with subtitles, or dubbed?

• Many people think that most film adaptations of books are very limited. Would you agree?

• Do you think that English language films should have limited distribution in other countries to help promote a local national film industry in each country?

• Many companies place their products in films as a way of indirectly advertising them. Do you think this practice should be banned?

1 Introduction

A How much do you know about prehistoric humans? Discuss these questions with a partner.

- Where did they live?
- How did they communicate?
- What did they look like?
- What could and couldn't they do?

B Scan the text below to find the answers to Questions 1 and 2. Which question is not answered in the text?

1 How do scientists date the time when humans first began speaking?

2 Why did early humans begin to speak?

Our growing brains

In the following extract from a text about the growth of the human brain and the development of language, the writer argues that in the light of new evidence, some previously held ideas need to be re-examined.

Anthropologists and fossil experts who accept that speech started early, still perceive language evolution as a gradual two-million-year process, with our own species, *Homo sapiens*, way out in front of our older ancestors. A major reason for this is the perception that brain growth among humans was gradual over the same 2.5m year period. However, several recent developments in fossil research bring this into doubt.

The first of these developments is a re-dating of soil layers from the famous Olduvai Gorge in east Africa where many key fossil remains have been found. A number of big-brained human species appear to be much older than previously thought, with several specimens dating over a million years old. When brain sizes for all available skulls are plotted against time using the revised dates, the result is startling: the significant increase in brain size was over by around 1.2 million years ago, with some African human species already having brain volumes easily within the modern human range. Our own African ancestors' brains stopped growing perhaps 200,000 years ago and even started shrinking over the past 150,000 years, the period of our own species' time on Earth.

So we have the paradox that over the period when our brain was growing most rapidly, our cultural development, as measured by stone tools, advanced only marginally. Then, over a million years later, when the culture of anatomically modern humans finally started to accelerate, artistically and technologically, our brains were actually getting smaller.

Source: *Out of Eden: The Peopling of the World* by Stephen Oppenheimer

IN THE EXAM

Reading module: True/False/Not given

Some Reading module tasks test your ability to follow the argument of a text and understand the author's opinion in depth. True/False/Not given questions require you to do this by identifying if the statement agrees or disagrees with an argument in the text, or is not mentioned in the text at all.

Multiple-choice questions often test your understanding of the argument by asking you to identify which arguments are mentioned in a text. You may have to choose one option from a list of four, or sometimes several options from a longer list.

2 Identifying distracting information

Read the text again more carefully and answer the questions below.

A Look at Question 1 in the box below. There are three options to choose from to answer the question. Only one of the options appears in the text AND answers the question. The other two options contain distracting information that appears in the text but does not answer the question.

- Which options appear in the text but do not answer the question?
- Which option appears in the text and answers the question?

---

1 What new ideas do the fossil remains reveal?

a The modern *Homo sapiens* brain is often thought to be the result of a long period of gradual development over 2.5 million years.

b Over 1 million years ago our cultural development advanced relatively slowly.

c Some human brains actually got smaller as the species evolved.

B Some options will seem logical, but in fact they are not the correct answer because they are not mentioned in the text.

Look at Question 2 below. One option is true according to the text. The other two options contain distracting information which is not mentioned in the text.

- Which options seem logical but are not mentioned in the text?
- Which option appears in the text and answers the question?

---

2 Which argument does the writer state in the text?

a Rapid brain growth occurred as humans became less instinctive and more emotional in their thinking.

b Language evolved in order to make hunting more efficient.

c At the same time as humans were becoming more culturally advanced, their brains were shrinking.

---

3 Identifying arguments

A Skim the text on the next page and decide which of the following statements (1–4) are mentioned in the article.

1 We need words to think – without language we cannot think.

2 As our brains evolve, so will our communication skills.

3 Language developed from sounds which accompanied physical gesture.

4 Early language was used for communicating stories about hunting and survival.

LOOK WHO WAS TALKING

We began talking as early as 2.5m years ago, writes Stephen Oppenheimer. Is that what drove the growth of our brains?

1 When did we start talking to each other and how long did it take us to become so good at it? In the absence of palaeo-cassette recorders or a time machine, the enigma might seem insoluble, but analysis of recent evidence suggests we may have started talking as early as 2.5m years ago.

2 There is a polar divide on the issue of dating and linking thought, language and material culture. One view of language development, held by linguists such as Noam Chomsky and anthropologists such as Richard Klein, is that language, specifically the spoken word, appeared suddenly among modern humans between 35,000 and 50,000 years ago, and that the ability to speak words and use syntax was recently genetically hard-wired into our brains in a kind of language organ.

3 This view of language is associated with the old idea that logical thought is dependent on words, a concept originating with Plato and much in vogue in the 19th century: animals do not speak because they do not think. The advances in communication and abstract thought demonstrated by chimps put this theory in doubt.

4 The notion of a great leap forward in the quality of human thinking is further reflected in a common interpretation of the flowering of Upper Palaeolithic art in Europe. European cave paintings in Lascaux and Chauvet in France and carved figurines that have been dated to over 30,000 years ago are seen, according to this perspective, as the first stirrings of symbolic and abstract thought, and also of language.

5 The problem with using art as prehistoric evidence for the first human that could speak is that, quite apart from its validity, the further back one looks, the more chance the evidence for art itself would have perished.

6 An alternative to the Chomskian theory, is that language developed as a series of inventions. This was first suggested by the 18th-century philosopher Etienne Bonnot de Condillac. He argued that spoken language had developed out of gesture language (langage d'action) and that both were inventions arising initially from the simple association between action and object. The Condillac view, with some development, can be traced to the present day with the recent work of New Zealand psychologist Michael Corballis and others. The theory sees gesture language as arising originally among apes as sounds accompanying gestures. These sounds gradually became coded into words as the new skill drove its own evolution. Subsequently, coded words developed into deliberate, complex communication. The pressure of evolution promoted the development of an anatomy geared to speech – the larynx, vocal muscles and a specific part of the brain immediately next to that responsible for gestures.

7 This view, that spoken language was ultimately a cultural invention like tool-making, which then drove the biological evolution of the brain and vocal apparatus, seems obvious when you think of the development of different languages.

8 Languages have unique features. French, for example, clearly does not result from any biological aspect of being French but is the cultural possession of the French-speaking community. Each language evolves from one generation to the next, constantly adapting itself to cope with the learning biases of each new generation.

9 Several skull and spinal modifications relating to speech production (arched base of skull and enlargement of the channel for nerves to the tongue in early human fossils, a lopsided brain and changes in relative proportions of the brain) have all been used to shift speech way back to early humans 2.5m years ago or even earlier.

10 So, what was driving this change 2.5m years ago? The answer may have been staring us in the face. Namely, that not only were early humans communicating but their ancestor, a walking ape, had started the trend in this very useful skill. Around 2.5m years ago, the weather took a decided turn for the worse, becoming more variable, colder and dryer. The search for food became more taxing, and there would have been a real need to communicate more effectively and cope with the ever worsening environment in a cooperative way.

11 Speech, a complex system of oral communication, is the only inherited primate skill that would self-evidently benefit from a larger computer than that of a chimp. The maximum in brain size achieved by 1.2m years ago indicates that those early ancestors could already have been talking perfectly well. Our new Rolls Royce brain, developed to manipulate and organise complex symbolic aspects of speech internally, could now be turned to a variety of other tasks.

12 So what happened in the million gap years after that? Why did we take so long to get to the moon? Cultural evolution aided by communication and teaching is a cumulative interactive process. If each new generation invented just one new skill or idea and passed it on with the rest to their children and cousins, you could predict exactly the same curve of cultural advance as we see from the archaeological and historical record – first very slow, then faster and faster.

B Re-read the second paragraph which describes the views of linguists Chomsky and Klein.
- Which of the statements below *agree* with the views put forward?
- Which of the statements below *disagrees* with the views put forward?
- Which of the statements below is not mentioned in the paragraph?

1 Humans developed a neurological mechanism which enables them to speak.
2 Early language was used for hunting and communicating.
3 Language developed gradually.
4 Humans started speaking a relatively short time ago.

4 Multiple-choice questions with multiple answers

for this task

▶ You will need to select a number of options which all answer the question correctly.

▶ An option may be contained in the text, but may not be the answer to the question. Ask yourself: is it true according to the text? If the answer is 'yes', ask yourself

does it answer the question? If the answer is 'yes', choose this option as a correct answer.

▶ The options follow the same order as the relevant information in the text – use them to find your way around the text.

Homework =)

Questions 1–3
Choose **THREE** *letters A–F.*

Which **THREE** of the following points describe an alternative theory of language development to that put forward by Chomsky and Klein?

A Without words, we cannot think. ✗
B Prehistoric cave paintings indicate early thought and language.
C Language developed from sounds which complemented physical gesture.
D Language development is driven by cultural development.
E Harsh weather conditions made efficient communication more important.
F Early language created a stronger family unit.

1 ......C......
2 ......D......
3 ......E......

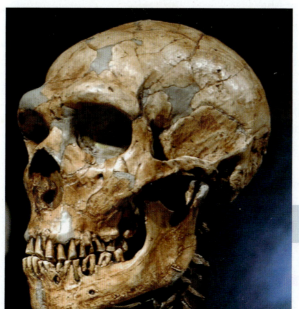

A reconstructed skull of a prehistoric human

5 Multiple-choice questions with single answers

for this task

▸ This task will usually focus on a particular section of the text. Scan the text to locate the relevant section. If there is more than one question, the questions will follow the order of the text.

▸ You may need to analyse very complex information, so you should read the relevant section of the text very carefully.

▸ As with multiple-answer questions, the option must be true according to the text and answer the question.

Questions 4–5

Choose the correct letter A, B, C or D.

express tip

The final question in the section will occasionally be a global question, which tests your understanding of the whole text.

4 Which of the following describes Michael Corballis's view of language development?

A Complex communication developed out of combinations of sounds and physical signs.

B Gesture language was essential for survival.

C Apes used complex language to help them make tools.

D The development of vocal apparatus allowed early apes to produce sounds accompanying gesture.

5 Which of the following does the author try to do?

A Explain how and why language developed much earlier than previously thought.

B Argue that rational thought emerged as a consequence of language development.

C Predict the future of language development.

D Compare early prehistoric skulls with those found more recently.

6 True/False/Not Given

for this task

▸ The questions follow the order of the the text. Locate the relevant part of the text quickly, then read the section carefully as you will need to absorb complex information.

▸ Pay attention to the difference between 'False' and 'Not given'. For an answer to be 'False', the information stated must make the statement incorrect. 'Not given' statements refer to information in the text, but do not show the statement to be true **or** false.

▸ For each answer, ask yourself the following questions:

• Is the point of view the same as the one in the text? (True)

• Is the point of view in the question opposite from the one in the text? (False)

• Is there no view on this in the text? (Not given)

Questions 6–11

Do the following statements agree with the information given in the reading passage?

Next to questions 6–11 write

TRUE if the statement agrees with the passage

FALSE if the statement contradicts the passage

NOT GIVEN if there is no information on this in the passage

6 Findings show that early humans could have been speaking 2.5 million years ago.   *TRUE*

7 Genetic variation in humans explains why we speak different languages.   *False*

8 The changing climate had a profound effect on language development.   *TRUE*

9 Climate change created different geographical landscapes.   *Not given*

10 Our brains were still growing 1.2 million years ago.   *False*

11 A fully developed brain allowed man to produce tools.   *Not given*

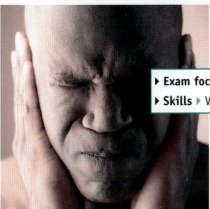

▸ **Exam focus** ▸ Speaking Part 2: Individual long turn; Speaking Part 3: Two-way discussion
▸ **Skills** ▸ Visualising the scene; hypothesising, speculating and evaluating

1 Introduction

How many of the following questions about language can you answer? Compare your answers with your partner.

1 Approximately how many languages are spoken in the world?
2 Which is the most widely spoken language in the world?
3 How many languages do you think will be spoken in 2100?
4 What percentage of the Internet is in English?
5 How many words do you think there are in the English language?

Check your answers with the answer key on page 115. Which answers do you find surprising?

2 Visualising the scene

In Part 2 of the Speaking exam, your talk will sound more interesting if you can 'see' what you are describing and explaining. Visualisation is a useful technique for doing this.

A Sit back, relax and close your eyes while your teacher asks you the questions on page 81. You don't need to answer the questions – just imagine!

B Now describe what you 'saw' to your partner and explain if you enjoyed the lesson or not. Were there any similarities in your answers?

IN THE EXAM

Speaking module Part 3: Two-way discussion

In this section of the exam, the examiner will ask different types of questions designed to further test your range of language. For example, you may be questioned about an imaginary situation, *What would happen if …?*, requiring you to hypothesise. Alternatively, you may be asked to evaluate something e.g. *Do you think ___ is a good thing or not?* The discussion lasts between 4 and 5 minutes.

3 Individual long turn

for this task

▶ Make brief notes on each point on the card. You should include keywords and expressions, and prompt words to jog your memory in case you get stuck.

▶ 1–2 minutes can seem like a long time: use the points on the card to help you stage and structure what you are going to say.

▶ Introduce your answer confidently – the first two or three seconds are the most crucial.

▶ Always keep your answer relevant to the topic on the card.

▶ Try to visualise the situation you are describing: it will help you provide more detail and make your answer more engaging.

▶ Remember to describe *and* explain. When you explain you should go into more depth and give a longer answer.

In pairs, practise the interview for two minutes each.

Student A: You are the candidate. For one minute look at the topic card below and make notes. Then, use your notes to speak for between one and two minutes. Follow the advice in the *for this task* box above.

Student B: You are the examiner. Give Student A one minute to look at the card below and make notes. Then listen to Student A's answer carefully. Does he or she follow the advice in the *for this task* box? After one or two minutes, interrupt and ask Student A one or two questions related to the topic to round off. When you have finished, change roles.

express tip

Practise as much as you can before the exam – on your own, with a friend, or in front of a mirror.

> **Describe an occasion when you found it difficult to understand something in English.**
> **You should say:**
>   **where you were**
>   **what/who you were reading or listening to**
>   **what you didn't understand**
> **and explain whether the lack of understanding was a problem and how you dealt with it.**

4 Hypothesising, speculating and evaluating

In Part 3 of the exam you will be asked to express your opinion on topics related to the subject you discussed in Part 2.

A A topic question can be expressed in different ways. Look at the following questions. They are about the topic of a single global language, but the question types are very different.

> 1 English is becoming increasingly dominant as a global language. Do you think this is a good thing?
> 2 Do you think the world will speak only one language in the future?
> 3 How would the world be different if everyone spoke the same language?

Which question asks you to:

hypothesise (talk about an imaginary situation)? ....

speculate (talk about how you think things might be in the future)? ....

evaluate (discuss the advantages and disadvantages of something and express an opinion)? ....

B 🎧 **7.1** Listen to some candidates discussing two of the questions in 4A. Complete the sentences below.

1 I think ...., we can do business more efficiently, but .... other languages may die out, so .... we need to monitor the situation more closely ...

2 I suppose .... the same language, it .... to do international business ...

3 In my opinion, political leaders .... to relate to each other better ...

C Discuss Questions A1 and A2 with a partner. Use language for speculation and evaluation.

5 Two-way discussion

for this task

▸ Show that you can discuss things beyond your personal experience. You should justify your opinion – say what you think and why you think it.

▸ Introduce your opinion with a variety of language – not only, *I think* … . Instead use, *In my opinion* … or *I believe* … .

▸ Listen for questions which ask you to compare and contrast two different things, speculate about the future, talk about a hypothetical situation or evaluate something. Then use the appropriate language to answer.

▸ Decide how to answer, then organise your ideas for a second or two in your mind before you start to speak.

▸ Say *OK* … or *Well* … to show the examiner that you are thinking – but don't wait too long before you speak!

▸ Take the initiative in the conversation and add extra information yourself.

Work in pairs. Practise the two-way discussion.

Student A: You are the examiner. Interview Student B for about 4–5 minutes. Ask some of the questions in the list below. Try to choose questions from each category. You should begin by saying, *We've been talking about language and communication, I'd like to discuss with you some further questions related to this topic* … . Listen to the answers carefully. Did Student B follow the advice in the *for this task* box? Use the examiner's assessment criteria to say how well they did or what they need to work on, i.e. fluency and coherence, lexical resource, grammatical range and accuracy, and pronunciation.

Student B: You are the candidate. You should answer the questions Student A asks you, following the advice in the *for this task* box. When you have finished, change roles.

Families and communication

• Do families communicate with each other more or less than they did in the past?

• How important is it that families can communicate with each other?

• What are some of the effects of family communication breakdown?

Politicians and lies

• Do politicians usually tell the truth in your country?

• Should politicians who are caught lying be banned from public office?

• What do you think would happen if all politicians told the truth?

2 Visualising the scene: questions

Imagine you are in a classroom in school, but not school today, think back to when you were a small child. What can you see? What does the classroom look like? Does it have big windows? What can you see on the walls? Can you see any pictures or perhaps some work done by students? Do you like this classroom?

How many children are in the classroom? Who is sitting next to you? Do you enjoy working with this person? Who is your teacher? Is he or she a good teacher? Do you like him or her? Why?

What subject are you studying? Are you enjoying the lesson? Or are you bored? Why?

8 Growth and Development

> ▶ **Exam tasks** ▶ Short-answer questions; multiple-choice with multiple answers; summary completion
> ▶ **Exam focus** ▶ Listening Section 4: Academic monologue
> ▶ **Skills** ▶ Identifying features of speech; using features of speech

1 Introduction

- Look at the three pictures above. How old do you think the baby is in each picture?
- Whilst in the womb, there are three different stages of development. What do you think they are?
- At what age can babies walk? What do you think are the stages of learning to walk?

2 Identifying features of speech

When we speak, our meaning is communicated not only by our choice of words, but also by the *way* we say them. Therefore, when listening, it's important to be able to recognise what 'message' is being conveyed through the pace, stress and intonation of the voice.

A Look at the features of speech described below. Complete each sentence with one word.

1 When talking about important things, a speaker's .... will often slow down.

2 A speaker will often .... important words.

3 A speaker may .... before and/or after an important point.

 B ⬤ **8.1** Listen to the first part of a talk on pre-natal development. As you listen, underline the parts of the talk where the speaker speaks faster than usual. The first sentence has been done as an example.

> For the majority of animals, <u>and I include human beings in this category</u>, the most dramatic physical changes actually happen before the organism is born. Is this really the case? Well, think about it! A mature adult human does not look that different to a newborn baby, but a newborn baby looks nothing like a fertilised egg.

IN THE EXAM

Listening Section 4: Academic monologue

Section four of the Listening Exam is an academic monologue. It features one speaker giving a talk or lecture of general academic interest.

Various task-types may appear, but common ones are summary completion, short-answer questions and multiple-choice with multiple answers.

C **8.1** Listen again twice. Each time listen for the following features of speech and mark them on the script.

Stress ▸ circle those words which are given particular stress
Pause ▸ put a slash (/) where the speaker pauses

Why does the speaker adjust their speech in this way? Discuss with a partner.

3 Using features of speech

A Look at the tapescript below with a partner. Can you predict where the speaker will pause, change pace or stress words? Try reading it out to each other. Mark your predictions on the script.

> For that is what we are at the time of our conception – a tiny, microscopic fertilised egg. Quite amazing, isn't it? In the following nine months before our birth, not only do we grow hundreds of times in size, but we go through three distinct stages of development. The first, as I have just mentioned, is the fertilised egg. Then around a fortnight after conception, the egg begins to repeatedly divide itself to become a mass of cells, known as the embryo. Two months later, this embryo has grown to approximately 2cm long and is referred to as a foetus.

8.2 Listen and check your predictions.

B Read this summary of the second part of the talk.

At conception, the 'baby' is a minute fertilised **1** ......egg......... . Whilst inside the mother, the baby has **2** ..distinct.... developmental stages of which this is the first. After two weeks it divides into a **3** ..mass of.... called the embryo. After two more months, the embryo is about 2cm long and is called a foetus. *Cells.*

a Compare the summary with what the speaker actually said in Section A. What information has been omitted from the summary? How many synonyms or paraphrases can you find?

b Complete the summary, using no more than three words for each answer.

C **8.2** Listen again and look at your completed summary. With a partner, discuss how features of speech help you to answer summary completion questions. Was the information you needed stressed or not? What about pace: was the information delivered quickly or slowly? When did the speaker pause? Does word stress correspond with an answer?

D **8.3** Listen to the final part of the talk and complete the summary on the next page, using no more than two words for each gap.

Three months after conception, the foetus is about **4** ....**8 cm**.... long, has arms and legs and looks a bit like a miniature **5** ..**Baby**.... . Seven months after conception, it is about 40cm long, has a fully developed system of reflexes and can breathe, swallow and **6** ...**cry**........ . So, if a baby is born prematurely, it stands a good chance of surviving.

E **8.4** Look at this example of a multiple-choice question with multiple answers. Listen to the recording and answer Questions 1–4. Pay particular attention to features of speech to help you answer the questions.

<table>
<tr><td>

express tip

Don't forget that some distractors may be stressed too.

</td><td>

Questions 1–4
Choose four letters **A–G.**
Which **FOUR** *things can* <u>newborn babies</u> *do?*

1 ......**B**........
2 ......**D**........
3 ......**E**........
4 ......**F**........

</td></tr>
</table>

A crawl
B identify certain smells
C recognise faces across the room
D smile
E swim
F turn their heads
G turn over

4 Short-answer questions

for this task

Short-answer question tasks ask you to give one or more answers to one question. There is a restriction on the number of words you can use, and you can only use words you hear on the recording.

As you listen
▶ Write your answers as you listen, in any order. Be prepared to change your answer if you hear a more suitable one later.

Before you listen
▶ Read the instructions carefully. How many words should you use for each answer?
▶ Read the question and identify keywords.

After you listen
▶ Check that your choices answer the question.
▶ Make sure you have not exceeded the word limit and remember to check your spelling.

8.5 **Questions 1–3**
List **THREE** parts of the body whose <u>change is crucial in growing infants</u> according to the Neuromuscular Maturation theory of motor development.

Write **NO MORE THAN TWO WORDS** *for each answer.*

1 ....**brain**,....
2 ..**muscles**.....
3 ....**growing skeleton**....

5 Multiple-choice with multiple answers

for this task

Multiple-choice questions may require you to select one correct answer from a choice of three options, or two from five, or four from seven. All multiple-choice questions should be approached in the same way. (See Unit 2.)

Before you listen

▶ Read the instructions carefully. How many options should you choose?

As you listen

▶ Listen for keywords and any synonyms, and take care to listen for features of speech to help you recognise the answer.

▶ You may hear several distractors. Make sure that your choice is the correct answer.

▶ Write your answers as you listen, as two or three answers can come quite close together.

 8.6 **Questions 4–7**

Choose **FOUR** letters **A–G**.

According to the Dynamic Systems Approach, which FOUR factors are crucial for a child to walk?

A ability to hold onto things

B ability to swim

C increased perceptual awareness

D motivation to go somewhere

E slimmed down body proportions

F sufficient muscular strength

G the stepping reflex

4 .... F

5 .... E

6 .... D

7 C

6 Summary completion

for this task

Summary completion questions require you to complete a summary of a section of the listening passage. The answers must be in the same form as on the recording. The number of words you can use in your answer is given in the rubric.

Before you listen

▶ Read the instructions carefully. How many words can you use?

As you listen

▶ Listen for keywords, synonyms and features of speech to help you locate the answer.

▶ Write your answers as you listen. Sometimes two or three answers will come quite close together. Don't worry about making your writing neat; you can write the answers neatly when you transfer them to the answer sheet at the end of the exam.

After you listen

▶ Make sure you have not exceeded the word limit and remember to check your spelling.

 8.7 **Questions 8–10**

Complete the summary below.

Write **NO MORE THAN TWO WORDS** for each answer.

8. world   10 body parts.
9 — The environment.

In the Perception–Action approach there is a strong correlation between our perception of our surrounding **8** .... and our ability to move within it. In order to plan and perform an action successfully, we must have information about our bodies, **9** .... and the relationship between the two. Perceptual information is also acquired by moving different **10** .... Actions generate further information for perceptual systems.

▸ **Exam Task** ▸ 'For and against' essay
▸ **Exam focus** ▸ Academic Writing Task 2
▸ **Skills** ▸ Deciding the approach; providing supporting evidence

1 Introduction

A What are the different age groups shown in the photos above?

B Listed below are some of the advantages of middle age. What might some disadvantages be?

Advantages	Disadvantages
• financial security	....
• good career	....
• material comforts	....
• enjoy family life	....

C With a partner, note down some advantages and disadvantages of being a teenager.

2 Deciding the approach

express tip

In an argument-led essay, do not state your opinion in the opening paragraph, just introduce the topic.

A Read the following four exam questions and decide which ones should be answered using an argument-led approach (discussing both sides of the argument equally) and which can be answered using a thesis-led approach (taking one side of the argument). Note that some questions can take both approaches.

1 *The generation gap between older and younger people in most countries in the world is simply too wide to be bridged.*
    To what extent do you agree or disagree?

2 *Some people view teenage conflict with their parents as a necessary part of growing up, whilst others view it as something negative which should be avoided.*
    Discuss both views and give your own opinion.

3 *Parents with undisciplined children should be made to follow compulsory 'parenting skills' classes where they can learn from professional teachers how to be good parents.*
    Do the advantages of this approach outweigh the disadvantages?

IN THE EXAM

Writing Task 2 requires a more in-depth and detailed answer than Task 1 and is therefore allocated two thirds of the overall mark for the Writing paper. You should therefore spend two thirds of the allocated time (40 minutes) completing this task.

Whereas in Task 1 you are asked to describe factual information presented to you, in Task 2 you are presented with a problem, a point of view or a controversial statement about a topic of general interest. You will need to analyse, explore and possibly challenge this statement, coming up with your own ideas. You should support your arguments with material based on your general knowledge and personal experience.

express tip

In a thesis-led essay, state your opinion in the opening paragraph; in an argument-led essay, use the conclusion to write your own personal opinion.

4 *Research into ways to bridge the generation gap has focused on having parents and their children living each other's lives for a day. This has involved exchanging daily routines inside and outside the home for 24 hours.*

What are the advantages and disadvantages of this approach?

Look at your choices and discuss with a partner how you decided between an argument-led question and a thesis-led question.

B Read the following two opening paragraphs.

a In my view, learning how to be a better parent can only be a good thing, and therefore I cannot see any real disadvantages. If parents feel they need or want these types of classes, and governments are able and willing to provide them, then surely it would bring positive benefits to parents, children and society in general.

b The 'generation gap' is an expression used to talk primarily about the lack of understanding between older and younger people, in particular between parents and teenage children. The question is, can this gap in understanding be bridged by following techniques which allow people from one generation to temporarily live the life of another? This essay will look at the advantages and disadvantages of using this method.

1 Which paragraph shows a thesis-led approach? Which one shows an argument-led approach?
2 Match the paragraphs to the essay questions in 2A.
3 Identify the following phrases as belonging to an introduction for an argument-led essay (A) or a thesis-led essay (T). Write A or T next to each one.

I believe   In my opinion   Many people think   It is generally considered that   I totally disagree with

C Now write an opening paragraph to answer Question 1 in 2A using the argument-led approach.

3 Providing supporting evidence

A Read the first paragraph of the main body of an argument-led essay below. Which essay question from 2A does it answer?

Some people argue that the generation gap is too wide because people from different generations have very different experiences of the world around them. **1** .... technology, which is used very differently by different generations. Young people **2** .... have been brought up with the Internet, email and text messaging as a very normal part of their lives, **3** .... older people who knew life before the Internet. **4** .... people in this age group are slower at leaning new technologies, which is very frustrating. My parents' situation **5** .... as they take a very long time to send text messages and still haven't learnt how to program the VCR yet!

B Complete the paragraph with these phrases for presenting supporting evidence.

> highlights the point   for instance
> from my experience   but this is not the case for
> a good example of this is

C Re-read the paragraph and note down the main idea of the paragraph and the supporting information.

Main idea	Supporting information
....	1 ....
	2 ....
	3 ....

D Write the next paragraph of the essay based on the following paragraph plan.

Main idea	Supporting information
different generations like to keep distance	• parents/bosses want respect • children/employees want privacy and fear judgement

E From the notes below, match the supporting information to the main ideas.

Main idea	Supporting information
1 parents/teenagers share similar attitudes/interests 2 parents show understanding of teenage children	a parents well informed on teenage issues b common values – e.g. importance of career c parents are yesterday's teenagers – experienced same problems d young and old enjoy spectator sports together e.g. football, baseball

F To complete the main body of this argument-led essay, write the next two the paragraphs based on the notes in 3E above. Start your first paragraph with:

On the other hand ...

4 Academic Writing Task 2: Essay

for this task

▶ Read the question carefully and decide whether you need to use an argument-led or thesis-led approach. In the exam question below you will need to use an argument-led approach.

▶ Underline keywords in the exam question to help you focus your answer on the key points, then brainstorm ideas for both sides of the argument, i.e. for and against the issue.

▶ Write a paragraph plan for the main body of the essay showing clear links between the main argument and the supporting arguments. Remember each paragraph should have one main argument – start a new paragraph when you start a new main idea.

▶ Re-word the question in your introduction showing the topic clearly. State the opinion(s) that you will go on to discuss.

▶ In the main body of the essay, use appropriate linking expressions (e.g. *From my experience* ...) to connect evidence from supporting arguments to the main argument. Paragraphs should also be linked to each other using relevant linking expressions, such as *on the other hand ... and turning to ...*

▶ Conclude your essay by summarising your main points and stating your own personal view.

You should spend about 40 minutes on this task.

Write about the following topic:

Some people view conflict between teenagers and parents as a necessary part of growing up, while others view it as something negative which should be avoided.

Discuss both views and give your own opinion.

Give reasons for your answers and include any relevant examples from your own knowledge or experience.

Write at least 250 words.

Questions 1–10

Questions 1–8

Complete the form below.

Write **NO MORE THAN THREE WORDS AND/OR A NUMBER** for each answer.

Cosmic Mail Order
Home Delivery Order Form

Name:	Alexandra **1** *Hornby*
Address:	28 Wood Road, **2** *Ilford*, Northchester, NC1 2FR
Account number:	**3** *944 567 81*
Item ordered:	**4** *Coffee table or a table*
Price (£):	**5** *39.99*
Free gift selected:	**6** *a hand bag*
Discount voucher code:	**7** *D.br29*
Delivery option:	**8** *express* service

Questions 9–10

For each question, choose **TWO** letters **A–E**.

9   In which **TWO** ways did Alexandra hear about Cosmic Mail Order?
   - A   Internet search
   - B   leaflet through the door
   - C   newspaper advertisement
   - D   personal recommendation
   - E   TV advertisement

10   Which **TWO** promotional offers are attractive to Alexandra?
   - A   cheap air flights
   - B   discount on mobile phone bills
   - C   free cinema tickets
   - D   half-price meals at restaurants
   - E   reductions at tourist attractions

Questions 11–20

Questions 11–15

Complete the diagram below.

Write **NO MORE THAN THREE WORDS** for each answer.

RACE PREPARATION

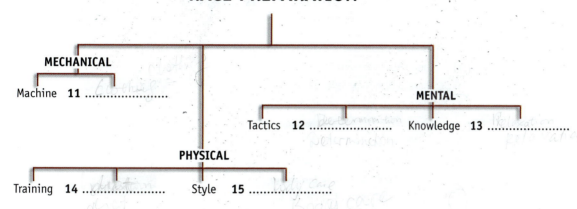

MECHANICAL

Machine **11** ....

Tactics **12** ....   Knowledge **13** ....

MENTAL

PHYSICAL

Training **14** ....   Style **15** ....

Questions 16–20

When should the following activities take place?

A   in summer ✓

B   in winter

C   all year round

Write the correct letter, **A**, **B**, or **C** next to questions 16–20.

16   circuit training ✓   ....

17   weight training   ....

18   mobility   ....

19   pleasure riding   ....

20   running   ....

Questions 21–30

Questions 21–23

List **THREE** sources of information the students agree they need to check.

Write **NO MORE THAN THREE WORDS** for each answer.

Questions 24–25

Choose the correct letter, **A**, **B**, or **C**.

24 What is Jane's concern about the information they will collect?
- A They will not evaluate it effectively.
- B There will not be enough of it.
- C Some of it will be unreliable.

25 What is Mark's concern about their assignment?
- A The assessment criteria are not clear.
- B Too much emphasis is placed on facts.
- C There is not enough time to do it well.

Questions 26–30

Complete the table below.

Write **NO MORE THAN ONE WORD** for each answer.

Cures for failing films

Name of cure	Reason for using cure
'Tweak every joke'	successful jokes increase film's 26 ....
'Change the ending'	difficult to predict audience's 27 ....
'Fix the tone'	important to be 28 ....
29 '.....................'	extra cost seen as investment
'Shift the 30 ....'	may attract a wider audience

Questions 31–40

Questions 31–37

Complete the sentences below.

Write NO MORE THAN THREE WORDS for each answer.

History of the Mediterranean Sea

The Roman influence

Estoren

31 Alexander the Great's death was followed by power struggles among rivals concerning the ......*Eastern*......... Mediterranean.

32 The Romans experienced the threat of ......*Piracy*.......... to their early naval supremacy.

33 The Roman Empire's first step in achieving naval supremacy was setting up a department for ......*repairing*........... ships.

34 The number of ......*slaves*........... meant that Roman warships were the fastest.

35 Growing Roman success was displayed by the number of ......*larg*........ *houses*........ that were built on the coast.   *salt*

36 Facilities in Spain were used to produce ......*fish source*........, which was exported throughout the Roman Empire.   *or sauce*

37 The development of a range of ......*specialiced*........... ships increased efficiency.

Questions 38–40

Quasetions 38 - 40

Views of Mediterranean history

Which view has been expressed by each historian of the Mediterranean?

Choose your answers from the box and write the letters A–F next to questions 38–40.

A National politics have strongly influenced the Mediterranean's history.   C
B The history of the Mediterranean needs to be understood in relation to other seas.   A
C The physical geography of the Mediterranean has determined its peoples' behaviour.   B
D Ecological change has been the biggest influence on the history of the Mediterranean.
E Sea access enabled distant societies to interact culturally around the Mediterranean.   B
F Exchanging raw materials around the Mediterranean linked countries together.   B

38 Michel Balard   B

39 Fernand Braudel   C

40 Nicholas Horden   D

You should spend about 20 minutes on **Questions 1–13** which are based on Reading Passage 1 below.

THE TREASURE HUNTERS

The contribution made to the preservation of Britain's heritage by 'detectorists' – amateur archaeologists who walk fields with metal detectors

1 On a raw November morning, Cliff Bradshaw was working a potato field in Kent with his metal detector when he heard a faint, high-pitched whine through his earphones. 'It was the tiniest possible signal,' he says. 'I knew it couldn't be iron because the machine would have made a growling noise. I scuffed the ground with my foot and tried again. The sound became more and more high-pitched as I dug down until it was shrieking in my earphones.'

2 Three weeks earlier he had found a rare seventh century gold coin on the same site, then four spindle whorls, followed by a silver strap-end from a Saxon belt and a gilded Saxon button-brooch. Yet he felt this was going to be different. More than a foot below the surface, he saw the gleam of what could only be gold. Buried silver goes grey, bronze goes green and iron turns rusty, but gold comes out of the ground as brilliant as the day it went in. As a symbol of permanence, there's nothing like it. That is its magic – for the metalworker, for the collector, for kings, for lovers, for treasure-hunters.

3 Bradshaw threw his excavating spade to one side and scraped with his hands until he had exposed the whole object. It was a corrugated cup made of sheet gold, savagely crushed on one side where it had been struck by a subsoiling machine, but still beautiful. There were tiny dots all around the rim and it had a broad, decorated handle secured with lozenge-shaped washers. Because of its round base, in its crumpled state it looked like a misshapen heart.

4 'I knew it was gold. I knew it was old. But there was no real jump for joy,' says Bradshaw. 'I never sell my stuff and I honestly didn't think about the money. I was just shocked. The real excitement for me was finding the prehistoric barrow where I was detecting – just a foot or so

of raised earth that was once as high as a house. It was difficult to see. No one had noticed it before.'

5 As he drove home with the cup, Bradshaw had a feeling that he had seen an object like it in one of his archaeological books. He found what he was looking for; his cup was so similar to the gold Rillington Cup, found in Cornwall in 1837 by a tin worker, that it might almost have been made by the same man. 'Bronze Age. Wow! It was like the find of three lifetimes. What I felt was wonderment more than excitement.'

6 He reported his find to an archaeologist, Keith Parfitt, who had good relations with local metal detectorists. Bradshaw's discovery is now famed as the Ringlemere Cup, only the second example in Britain of an Early Bronze Age gold cup. It dates from between 1700 and 1500 BC. Because the cup was more than 300 years old and made of more than 10% gold, it qualified as treasure under the 1996 Treasure Act, and a reward of £270,000 reflecting its value was divided equally between Bradshaw and the farmer whose land he had been exploring. Professional excavations, with Bradshaw as part of the team, will continue on the site for many years, yielding up more artefacts; more information about society in prehistoric Britain. 'It's being called a ritual landscape,' he says. 'The floor our ancestors walked on. You can't put a value on that, can you?'

7 This is how archaeologists and museum curators would like every story of amateur treasure finds to end. But they don't. An astonishing 90 per cent of all 'treasure' in Britain is uncovered by 'detectorists', as they like to be known, sweeping the fields and hedgerows with metal detectors. The hobby took off in the 1970s and is now practised by some 30,000 enthusiasts, often in

wretched wintry conditions when agricultural land is fallow. Most of them do it because, like Bradshaw, they love the sense of 'being in touch with the past' and have become knowledgeable spare-time archaeologists in their own right. But a few are blatantly in it for the money and some sites have been wrecked beyond recovery by their depredations. Without an accurate 'findspot', an exact provenance, all treasure is devalued and archaeology loses the vital context it needs for an object to have real meaning.

8 Relations between the professionals and the amateurs have often been hostile, archaeologists regarding nasty metal detectorists as ignorant plunderers and detectorists resenting snooty archaeologists as high-handed and obstructive. Helped by the act, which encourages people to declare their finds by offering a reward determined by a panel of experts, and by the contribution metal detecting obviously makes to our heritage, the two groups have reached a state of respectful co-operation.

Richard Hobbs, the British Museum's expert in prehistory and early Europe, says it all comes down to individuals. Some report everything, some will be tempted to slip a gold coin into their boot. There are plenty of discreet outlets for stolen antiquities. 'Some countries have a complete ban on metal detectorists or treat them harshly,' he says. 'But we are all after the same thing. These objects don't belong to any of us. Hopefully, we are all rowing in the same direction.'

9 This certainly wasn't true in the 1980s in Wanborough, Surrey, where the site of a Romano-Celtic temple was plundered by detectorist 'nighthawks' from all over the country. The looting and wrecking of Wanborough was a turning point. It worsened relationships between amateurs and professionals – but it helped push through the new treasure legislation of 1996.

Questions 1–3

Label the diagram below.

Choose **NO MORE THAN THREE WORDS** from the passage for each answer.

Write your answers next to questions 1–3.

CLIFF BRADSHAW'S FIND

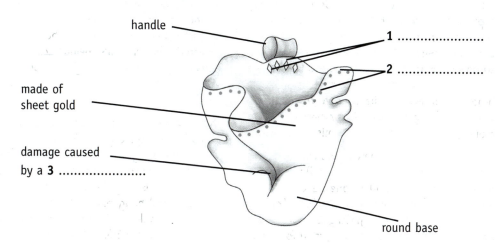

handle

1 ....

2 ....

made of
sheet gold

damage caused
by a 3 ....

round base

Questions 4–10

Complete the flow chart below.

Choose **NO MORE THAN THREE WORDS** from the passage for each answer.

The events of Cliff Bradshaw's find

Cup is found using a metal detector and an **4** ...., where Cliff Bradshaw was detecting in a **5** ....

↓

Bradshaw notes that it resembles a cup that was discovered by **6** .... in 1837.

↓

Bradshaw informs a local archaeologist of his find.

↓

Bradshaw's find is named **7** ....

↓

Because of its age and content the cup is legally declared to be **8** ....

↓

Bradshaw shares the reward with **9** ....

↓

Professional excavations continue on the site.

↓

The site is now regarded as a **10** ....

Questions 11–13

*Choose the correct letter, **A**, **B**, **C** or **D**.*

Write your answers next to 11–13.

11 What is said about detectorists in the seventh paragraph?

    A Most of them are not serious about the hobby.

    B Some of them have caused serious damage.

    C Some of them think that the name is inappropriate.

    D Most of them do research before taking up the hobby.

12 What is said about relations between archaeologists and detectorists?

    A Mutual tolerance now exists between the two groups.

    B Relations have changed because the two groups have been forced to work together more closely.

    C There is still some ill feeling between the two groups.

    D Archaeologists began the process of improving the relationship between the two groups.

13 Which of the following does Richard Hobbs believe?

    A Attitudes towards detectorists are changing everywhere.

    B Competition between detectorists can cause problems.

    C Laws against detectorists tend to be ineffective.

    D There may still be some dishonest detectorists.

*You should spend about 20 minutes on **Questions 14–26** which are based on Reading Passage 2 below.*

ONLY THE EAGLE-EYED WILL SPOT A FAKE

1 Do natural history programmes distort reality? Of course they do. Go for a walk in a tropical rainforest after watching a programme about one and you will be in no doubt of that. On television, all kinds of animals appear continuously all over the place. In reality, you may be lucky to see a single bird or monkey.

2 But are there distortions that are more serious than that? Does it matter that a programme about the life of a polar bear, filmed for the most part in the Arctic, includes shots of a mother bear giving birth that were taken in a zoo – and that the commentary did not say so? That depends on the programme. If the programme claimed to be recording the actual adventures of an Arctic explorer, then that would clearly be wrong. But if its aim is to document the life history of the polar bear, then I believe that could be acceptable. Filming a polar bear birth in the wild is virtually impossible. Trying to do so might well endanger the lives of both the cameraman and the cub, were the mother to be disturbed. So the only way to include shots of that crucial event in a bear's life is to film it in captivity.

3 Is it acceptable – on occasion – to use film to suggest that something happened which did not? Sometimes it is. That swoop by a peregrine falcon did not, in fact, result in the death of a grouse. The puff of feathers rising into the sky was thrown into the air by one of the film crew. With such a shot at his disposal, the skilful film editor was able to create a sequence representing a successful peregrine hunt – without it costing the life of a bird.

4 But such stagings must be done with care. Sometimes a film shows an event that not only did not take place on that occasion, but has never happened – ever. The most notorious example comes not from television but from the cinema. Producers working on a natural history documentary for a well-known film studio made a film about the Arctic. Its highlight was a sequence featuring lemmings. Every few years, according to a widely believed story, lemming numbers increase to such an extent that the animals, swarming over the tundra, eventually deliberately commit suicide by swimming out to sea and drowning themselves. So the film team working in northern Canada paid local children to collect live lemmings. A few dozen were then taken down to an enclosure on the banks of a river and filmed in such a way that a few dozen appeared to be a plague. They were then chivvied until they came to the edge of the river bank and tumbled over it into the water. And the film-makers had their sequence.

5 The need for such tricks has, over the years, become less and less. Lenses have become more powerful. The large film cameras driven by clockwork that we had to use a few decades ago have been replaced by electronic cameras, some no bigger than a lipstick, that can be strapped to an eagle's back or lowered down a mouse-hole. We can now, with infra-red light, record what goes on in what appears to both animals and ourselves to be total darkness.

6 But, paradoxically, these huge advances in our ability to record reality have coincided with other developments that enable us to falsify more convincingly than ever. Just as

computer imaging can bring long-extinct dinosaurs back to life, so the same techniques could also make living animals appear to do things that a cameraman failed to film in reality – maybe because he was unlucky or because, in spite of what some book says, the animal in fact never behaves that way. We can now combine pictures so perfectly that a natural history presenter could appear to be crouching within a yard of a ferocious animal that he has never ever seen. That has not happened yet, as far as I know. It would be nice to say that if you or I looked closely enough, we could spot it. But electronic techniques are now so ingenious that such deceptions could be almost undetectable.

7 In these circumstances, television producers and the organisations which transmit their work have to guard their reputations for honesty with greater care than ever. The BBC Natural History Unit in Britain already has a code governing the treatment of animals during filming. The welfare of the subject is more important than the success of the film. There should be no lighting that makes it easier for one animal to hunt another. It also lays down rules about deceptions. Telling the story of an animal identified as an individual, but using shots of several, is now impermissible. Other tricks and techniques we have used in the past, no matter how well-intentioned, are no longer acceptable.

8 As film-makers trying to illuminate the natural world, we must be allowed to manipulate images and use all the devices that recent technological advances have given us. But we must also recognise our responsibilities to scientific truth. The events and the creatures we chronicle are more than just entertainment that can be jazzed up to taste.

Questions 14–21

Do the following statements agree with the views of the writer in Reading Passage 2?

Write

YES   if the statement agrees with the views of the writer

NO   if the statement contradicts the views of the writer

NOT GIVEN   if it is impossible to say what the writer thinks about this

14   It may be justifiable to pretend that a film was shot in a particular location.

15   It may be impossible to avoid showing a creature being killed.

16   Some film-makers have presented an accurate view of lemming behaviour.

17   There are more instances of falsehood in wildlife film-making now than there used to be.

18   Published accounts of animal behaviour may be incorrect.

19   It is possible that films have been made showing presenters nearer to animals than they really were.

20   Wildlife films made by the BBC have a higher reputation than those made by many other film-makers.

21   False impressions in wildlife films in the past were sometimes created for good reasons.

Questions 22–25

Complete each sentence with the correct ending **A–G** from the box below.

Write the correct letter **A–G** next to questions 22–25.

22 A programme about the tropical rainforest E

23 A programme about polar bears C

24 A film involving a bird of prey killing another bird G

25 A film involving an eagle in flight A

A is likely to have benefited from advances in technology.
B may show something that never really happens.
C may need to include material not filmed in the wild.
D is likely to be perceived as unrealistic by viewers.
E is likely to give a false impression of the amount of wildlife.
F may correct common but incorrect beliefs.
G may not actually show the event it pretends to show.

Question 26

Choose the correct letter, **A**, **B**, **C** or **D**.

Write your answer next to question 26.

26 What is the writer's main point in the passage as a whole?

    A More attention should be paid to the issue of the authenticity of wildlife films.

    B Advances in technology have created problems for wildlife film-makers who are concerned with the truth.

    C It is acceptable for wildlife film-makers to falsify images as long as they present accurate information.

    D The desire to entertain has begun to outweigh other considerations in wildlife film-making.

*You should spend about 20 minutes on **Questions 27–40** which are based on Reading Passage 3 below.*

HYPOCHONDRIA

Every doctor recognizes them. The man who discovers a bruise on his thigh and becomes convinced that it is leukemia. The woman who has suffered from heartburn all her life but after reading about esophageal cancer has no question that she has it. They make frequent doctor's appointments, demand unnecessary tests and can drive their friends and relatives – not to mention their physicians – to distraction with a seemingly endless search for reassurance. By some estimates, they may be responsible for 10 to 20 per cent of the United States's staggering annual health care costs.

Yet how we deal with hypochondria, a disorder that afflicts one of every twenty Americans who visit doctors, has been one of the most stubborn puzzles in medicine. Where the patient sees physical illness, the doctor sees a psychological problem, and frustration rules on both sides.

Recently, however, there has been a break in the impasse. New treatment strategies are offering the first hope since the ancient Greeks recognized hypochondria 24 centuries ago. Cognitive therapy, researchers report, helps hypochondriacal patients evaluate and change their distorted thoughts about illness. After six 90-minute therapy sessions, one study found, 55 per cent of the 102 participants were better able to do errands, drive and engage in social activities. In the study, the patients, whose fixation on illness had greatly interfered with their lives, did not see their symptoms disappear, but they did learn to pay less attention to them.

'The hope is that with effective treatment, a diagnosis of hypochondria will become a more acceptable diagnosis and less a laughing matter or a cause for embarrassment,' said Dr Arthur J Barsky, director of psychiatric research at Brigham and Women's Hospital in Boston. He is the lead author of the study on cognitive therapy, which appeared in the Journal of the American Medical Association.

An official diagnosis of hypochondria, according to the American Psychiatric Association, is reserved for patients whose fears that they have a serious disease persist for at least six months and continue even after doctors have reassured them that they are healthy. Researchers have found that hypochondria, which affects men and women equally, seems more likely to develop in people who have certain personality traits. The neurotic, the self-critical, the introverted and the narcissistic appear particularly prone to hypochondriacal fears, said Dr Michael Hollifield, an associate professor of psychiatry at the University of New Mexico.

Sometimes patients become so fearful about their imagined illness that they exacerbate the symptoms, 'A headache that you believe is due to a brain tumor is a lot worse than a headache you believe is due to eyestrain,' Dr Barsky said. In the most extreme cases, patients can worry to the point where they develop delusions or become almost entirely disabled by fear.

The ancient Greeks used the word 'hypochondria' to describe symptoms of digestive discomfort, combined with melancholy, that they thought originated in the organs of the hypochondrium, the region under the rib cage. The term applied only to men. In women, unexplained symptoms were attributed to hysteria, resulting from a misalignment of the uterus.

This view prevailed for 2,000 years, until the 17th century, when symptoms of hypochondria – digestive trouble, pain, convulsions, shortness of breath and heart palpitations – were seen as arising from the brain, set off by fear, grief and other feelings. Thomas Sydenham, an English physician, said that hypochondria in men and women should be considered the same affliction. Yet doctors could offer little in the way of treatment beyond the traditional strategies of bloodletting, sweating and inducing vomiting.

In the 18th century, George Cheyne, a Scottish physician, described hypochondria as 'the English malady', noting that it occurred mainly in people of high intelligence and members of the upper class, and was caused by moist air, variable weather, heavy food and sedentary living. But traditional treatments still prevailed. In the 19th century, hypochondria was viewed as melancholia, a term that covered everything from slight hypersensitivity to physical symptoms, delusions and suicidal tendencies. Treatment became more humane: spa visits for exercise, fresh air, nutritious food and relaxation. But some physicians still relied on old methods, including potions and elixirs.

In the 20th century, Freud recognized that hypochondria had both psychological and physical properties. Some doctors tried hypnosis and later pyschoanalysis to help patients uncover the psychological roots of their problem. But other doctors held that the suffering of hypochondriacs must be 'all in their heads'.

Today, just mentioning the word hypochondria to a patient, Dr Barsky said, can cause trouble. 'That comes across as, "You're telling me I'm a faker, a malingerer, that it's all in my head",' he said. 'It's tremendously pejorative.' Some experts have suggested that doctors drop the word altogether, substituting the term 'health anxiety', which has fewer negative connotations.

Questions 27–30

Do the following statements agree with the information given in Reading Passage 3?

Write your answer next to 27–30.

TRUE	if the statement agrees with the information
FALSE	if the statement contradicts the information
NOT GIVEN	if there is no information on this

27 Some illnesses are more commonly claimed by hypochondriacs than other illnesses. ....
28 The number of people suffering from hypochondria in the US has been rising. ....
29 Some patients in the study ceased to suffer from hypochondria after sessions. ....
30 Some sufferers may actually experience more pain because of their hypochondria. ....

Questions 31–34

Complete the summary below.

Choose **NO MORE THAN THREE WORDS** from the passage for each answer.

Write your answers next to 31–34.

Hypochondria — the current situation

A new treatment has emerged which seems to be a breakthrough. This is called
31 .... and it helps sufferers to deal with their hypochondria.
The American Psychiatric Association states that to be officially considered to be suffering
from hypochondria, a patient must have the symptoms for a minimum of **32** ....
Research indicates that the condition tends to affect people with particular **33** ....
Some patients dislike the term 'hypochondria' and some experts recommend that the
condition is referred to as **34** .... instead.

Questions 35–40

Classify the following facts about hypochondria as being true

A before the 17th century
B in the 17th century
C in the 18th century
D in the 19th century
E in the 20th century

Write the correct letter, **A–E** next to 35–40.

NB You may use any letter more than once.

35 It was believed to affect a certain section of society in particular.
36 There was disagreement among doctors on the cause of it.
37 It was considered to be caused by certain emotions.
38 The word was not used for everyone who had the same condition.
39 Both new and traditional treatments were in use.
40 Lack of exercise was identified as a contributory factor.

You should spend about 20 minutes on this task.

The bar charts below show changes in the monthly sales of new vehicles in the US over one year when compared with the previous year. The vehicles are in three categories – large SUVs (sports utility vehicles), large pick-ups (a kind of truck), and all other vehicles.

Summarise the information by selecting and reporting the main features, and make comparisons where relevant.

Write at least 150 words.

Changes in new vehicle sales from the previous year, plotted monthly

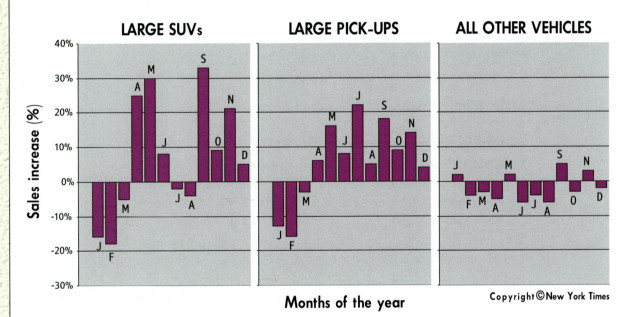

Copyright©New York Times

You should spend about 40 minutes on this task.

Write about the following topic:

> *Although modern life has brought with it improvements in people's standard of living, people are not generally happy with their lives.*
>
> *Do you agree or disagree?*

Give reasons for your answers and include any relevant examples from your own knowledge or experience.

You should write at least 250 words.

PART ONE

Example questions

• What are you studying?
• When did you decide to study that subject?
• What do you find most interesting about your subject?
• Do you enjoy being a student?
• Is there anything you don't like about your studies?

• Which newspapers and magazines do you read?
• Which parts of a newspaper do you think are most useful for people to read?
• How can reading newspapers and magazines help in learning English?
• Do you think that the Internet will replace newspapers and magazines?

• Do you play a musical instrument?
• What is your favourite kind of music?
• What kinds of music are the most popular where you live?
• Do you think it's better to listen to live music or recordings?

PART TWO

Example task

Read the topic card below carefully.

You will have to talk about the topic for one to two minutes.

You have one minute to think about what you are going to say.

You can make notes to help you if you wish.

Describe how you would like to spend a free day.
You should say:
   where you would spend the day
   what you would do during the day
   who you might like to spend the day with
and explain why you would like to spend the day like this.

PART THREE

Example questions

• Do you think that people generally have enough leisure time?
• What kinds of leisure activities do you think might be popular in the future?
• Do you think that education influences the ways people spend their leisure time?
• What effects on society do you think any changes in the retirement age might have?

WRITING BANK

ACADEMIC WRITING

▶ Task 1: Report (Unit 2)

Writing a report

▶▶ **Exam task**

You should spend about 20 minutes on this task.

The table shows the average band scores for students from different language groups taking the IELTS Academic Paper in 2003.

Summarise the information by selecting and reporting the main features, and make comparisons where relevant.

Write at least 150 words.

The language groups are listed in alphabetical order.

	Listening	Reading	Writing	Speaking	Overall
Hindi	6.78	6.38	6.62	6.86	6.73
Malayalam	6.31	6.13	6.49	6.52	6.43
Russian	6.35	6.13	6.11	6.69	6.38
Spanish	6.27	6.42	6.08	6.64	6.41

Source: www.ielts.org

Note that the question states 'language groups' NOT countries: Spanish speakers include people from Spain and countries in Latin America.

Useful phrases

Introduction
The table/diagram illustrates a breakdown of ...
The table/diagram shows the ... broken down into ...

Second Paragraph
From an overall perspective ...
Taking a general overview ...

Third Paragraph
Ranking other ... in order of ...
Moving to the other main points in the chart ...
We can see that/It can be seen that ...
Surprisingly ...

Conclusion
As a final point, it is interesting to note that ...
To conclude, it is worth pointing out that ...

In the introduction, state briefly what the table shows. DO NOT describe the information within the table.

The table illustrates the breakdown of scores for the IELTS Academic Paper in 2003. It shows separate scores for all four sections (Listening, Reading, Writing and Speaking), together with the overall score for students from four different language groups around the world.

Describe the main information in the table.

From an overall perspective, Hindi speakers achieved the highest grades with an average score of 6.73 across all four sections. Moreover, they scored the highest of all four language groups in three of the four sections (Listening, Writing and Speaking).

Describe the breakdown of information. Add any key details.

Malayalam speakers scored the second highest scores overall, closely followed by Spanish and Russian speakers. Although Malayalam speakers did not do so well in the Reading, Speaking and Listening sections compared to Russian and Spanish speakers, there was a significant difference in their grades for the Writing section. These grades were high relative to Russian and Spanish candidates. Surprisingly, Spanish speakers, who achieved the second lowest results overall, achieved the highest results of all four language groups for the Reading section.

Describe any interesting or unusual information. Provide a deeper interpretation of any figures not obviously apparent.

As a final point, it is interesting to note that the scores for each section show that all students on average scored the highest marks for the Speaking section and the lowest marks for the Reading section.

Thesis-led approach essay

▶▶ **Exam task**

You should spend about 40 minutes on this task.

Write about the following topic:

Most high-level positions in companies are filled by men even though the workforce in many developed countries is more than 50 per cent female. Companies should be required to allocate a certain percentage of these positions to women.

To what extent do you agree?

Give reasons for your answers and include any relevant examples from your own knowledge or experience.

Write at least 250 words.

Useful phrases

Introduction
I do not personally believe …
It is a fact that …
In this essay I will show that …

Giving an opinion
I believe …
To my mind, ….
It is my belief that …
It is a question of …
In my opinion …
It seems to me …

Refuting a point of view
To those who argue that …,
I … would like to point out that …
It might be argued that …, but …
I cannot accept this because …
It is a proven fact that …
Although there is …, I still feel that …

Conclusion
In summary …
In conclusion …
To sum up …
We have seen that …

Decide on the approach before you start: thesis-led or argument-led?

Repeat the ideas in the question, but do not copy the words and phrases.

In many countries these days, females make up over 50 per cent of the workforce, and increasingly highly-skilled women are taking managerial positions. However, it is still a fact that high positions such as CEO jobs are still dominated by men. Although this is not desirable, I do not personally believe that imposed quotas are the solution.

If you choose a thesis-led approach, make your opinion clear in the introduction.

Firstly, I believe companies have a right to choose the best person for the job, whatever their gender, in order to contribute to the success of their business. Forcing companies to hire, promote and appoint women could negatively affect business in the short term and even in the long term.

Support your ideas using a reason.

Secondly, to my mind the solution to this problem should be solved outside the workplace. Girls need to be encouraged to take more male-dominated subjects at school and later at university, and to aspire to do well in their careers. Girls and boys also need to be taught equality from an early age. This education can take place in schools, career programmes and in the home.

In the middle paragraphs present one point per paragraph to justify your opinion.

To those who argue that quotas are a good way to initiate this change, I would like to point out that artificially imposing rules has not always had the desired effect. When governments required males and females to receive the same pay for the same job, employers simply changed job titles to ensure that women were still paid less than men. It is my belief that employers will simply try to find loopholes to get around any such law.

Support your opinion with an example.

Show why you disagree with other points of view.

In summary, I do not believe that forcing companies to allocate jobs to women is the best way to address this imbalance. Rather, it is a question of education and of changing mindsets so that those who deserve to be at the top will earn it and be appropriately appointed.

Summarise your opinion from the introduction in different words. Do not include new information in the conclusion.

ACADEMIC WRITING

▶ Task 1: Report (Unit 6)

Describing charts and graphs

▶▶ **Exam task**

You should spend about 20 minutes on this task.

The diagram shows how a transaction works from an ATM (automated teller machine).

Summarise the information by selecting and reporting the main features, and make comparisons where relevant.

Write at least 150 words.

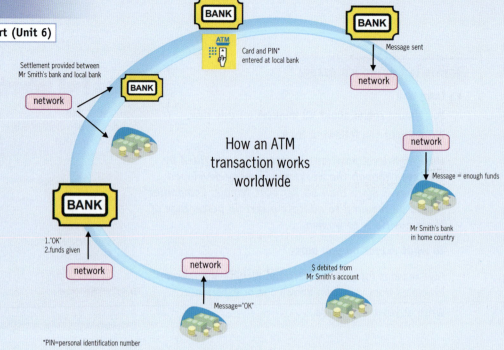

How an ATM transaction works worldwide

Card and PIN* entered at local bank

Message sent

network

network

Message = enough funds

Mr Smith's bank in home country

$ debited from Mr Smith's account

Message="OK"

Settlement provided between Mr Smith's bank and local bank

network

1."OK" 2.funds given

network

*PIN=personal identification number

Useful phrases

Introduction
The diagram/chart/table shows ...
In the diagram we can see ...
There are ... stages shown in this diagram.

Sequencing
First of all ...
The second thing that occurs is ...
Next ...
After that ...
As soon as ...
Finally ...
... (not) until ...

Outline the process in your introductory sentence.

Choose a logical place to start. Clearly define the stages using sequencing vocabulary.

Use the present passive where appropriate in process tasks.

Use the present simple in processes when you state the subject.

Summarise to finish off your essay.

The diagram shows how a transaction works at an automated teller machine in five steps, allowing us to withdraw money from any participating bank in the world.

First of all, Mr Smith inserts his card and PIN into the ATM at a local bank abroad. An electronic message is sent to the central network which is passed on to Mr Smith's own bank in his home country. The local bank will not dispense the cash until it knows the funds are available in Mr Smith's own account.

As soon as the home country bank receives the request and checks the balance, the money is debited from the account. The bank then replies to the message via the network, stating that the local bank can provide Mr Smith with the amount requested. Mr Smith retrieves the money and his card and goes on his way. Later that day a settlement occurs between the two banks facilitated by the central network.

This diagram shows the convenience of ATMs for the user and what goes on behind the scenes to ensure banks only provide money via their ATMs if the account holder has sufficient funds.

Argument-led approach essay

▸▸ **Exam task**

You should spend about 40 minutes on this task.

Write about the following topic:

shows the topic of discussion →

Some people view conflict between teenagers and parents as a necessary part of growing up, while others view it as something negative which should be avoided.

You will lose marks if you only discuss one side of the argument. →

Discuss both views and give your own opinion.

Give reasons for your answers and include any relevant examples from your own knowledge or experience.

Write at least 250 words.

shows TWO opposite views of the topic ⟩

Useful phrases

Introduction
The question is ...
The problem is ...
The issue is ...

Showing cause and effect
As a result of this ...
Owing to this ...
Due to this ...

Extending your argument
It should also be noted ...
It also needs to be taken into consideration that ...
In my personal case ...
From personal experience ...

Conclusion
Personally I think ...
In my opinion ...
In my view ...
From my own perspective ...

Use open questions to get the reader to think about the topic and decide which of the two views they agree more with.

We all want to grow up into mature and confident adults, who are emotionally and psychologically balanced. The question is – how can this be achieved? Do we encourage young people to rebel against their parents as a way of 'standing on their own two feet' and establishing their independence, or do we take the opposite view and discourage generational conflict between parents and children by helping both age groups to better understand each other?

State the topic of discussion and clearly show that there are two sides to the argument.

Adolescence is traditionally a difficult age when young people go through dramatic physical and emotional changes in a relatively short space of time. As a result, many people feel that some conflict between parents and their children is inevitable. In a sense, it is neither 'good' nor 'bad', it is just a fact of life. I think it should also be noted that 'conflict' is seen differently by different cultures – in the West it can often be seen in a positive light, whilst in many Asian cultures it has negative associations.

Extend your argument and provide examples.

Draw on your own personal experience.

In my own personal case, I didn't communicate very much with my parents while I was growing up and therefore there was no real conflict involved in our relationship, but on the other hand there was no real understanding either. This was a similar experience of many of my male friends. Girls, on the other hand, seemed to have a closer relationship with their mothers, especially the ones with younger mothers, which meant that the age gap was not so great.

Personally, I think that in an ideal world, children should communicate closely with their parents because both could learn a lot from each other. In my view, I think we isolate ourselves too much within the narrow confines of our own age group, giving us a limited view of the world and preventing us from growing up in the best way possible. The problem is, we don't live in an ideal world. Parents and their children are not perfect, so in the end I feel that teenage conflict is probably an inevitable, but certainly not negative, part of growing up.

Challenge the question by accepting one of the points of view and give your personal opinion.

1 Leisure Activities

READING

1 Introduction

B calm: relaxed, utterly unstressed

quite stressed: a little frustrated, pretty anxious, somewhat nervous, slightly edgy

stressed: really stressed out, incredibly uptight

2 Approaching the text

A Holidays can be stressful.

B Aimed at a general readership. You might see this article in a newspaper.

3 Skimming for main ideas

A Paragraph E: Now we have a formula to calculate the amount of holiday time needed to recover from the stress of preparing for what should be our annual period of rest and recuperation.

Paragraph F: Today's pressurised lifestyles mean that going on holiday is a lot more stressful.

Paragraph G: So according to Ms Quilliam, the secret to a stress-free holiday is planning and having realistic expectations.

Paragraph H: The results of a survey commissioned by Lloyds TSB bank and carried out by Ms Quilliam, have confirmed her theories; today's holidaymakers really are stressed out.

B 1 A: a; **B:** a; **C:** b; **D:** b

2 Suggested answers:

Paragraph E: There is a formula for calculating the number of hours needed on holiday to recover from the stress of organising the holiday.

Paragraph F: Today's complex holiday preparations mean holidays are more stressful than they used to be.

Paragraph G: If you plan carefully and do not have too high expectations you can have a stress-free holiday.

Paragraph H: A survey showed that most people get stressed on the run-up to their holiday.

C Paragraph A: Examples of travel arrangements

Paragraph C: Body needs time to regain balance

Paragraph D: Examples of psychological problems

Paragraph E: Explanation of the formula

Paragraph F: Examples of today's complex travel arrangements

Paragraph G: Examples of good planning

Paragraph H: Detailed breakdown of survey results

D Example: (P) 20 hours preparation X (S) 4 (slightly edgy) = 80 divided by (H) 10 (medium stress) = (R) 8 hours rest before enjoying the holiday

4 Scanning for keywords

A 1 fantasise, everyday grind; **2** expert; **3** more than a quarter

B 1 (long) break; **2** body language; **3** recover

C 1 swimming costume, formal clothes; **2** psychological symptoms; **3** research

The answers are:

1 reading material; **2** anxiety, irritability, mild depression; **3** Lloyds TSB bank

5 Matching headings to paragraphs

1 iii; **2** ii; **3** x; **4** ix; **5** vi; **6** vii; **7** v; **8** i

6 Summary completion

9 devised; **10** pressurised lifestyles; **11** realistic expectations; **12** (any) unfinished work; **13** tell their bosses

7 Short-answer questions

14 hormonal; **15** a formula; **16** bucket and spade; **17** severely stressed

SPEAKING

2 Giving personal information

1 Do you have any brothers or sisters?

2 Do you enjoy studying English?

3 Do you play any sport?

4 Have you got a job?

5 What do you plan to do after you finish your studies?

6 Where are you from?

7 What's your favourite subject?

3 Providing additional information

A 1 I really like playing with his children, but it's always good to give them back to him at the end of the day! When I'm older I'd like to have some children myself, maybe two boys and a girl. I think that having children ...

2 But it's very hard work and sometimes I feel like I don't get better, er ... I'm not making a lot of progress. I prefer studying economics, which is the subject I'm hoping to study when I go to university next year. You know, it's interesting to learn about ...

3 I got a new game recently – it's really great. You're a criminal and you have to drive your car really fast about a city, and then sometimes escape from the police. It's very exciting. Sometimes I play with my friends, but it's quite difficult to ...

4 It's very good because it gives me time to study and I meet people to practise my speaking, you know, talking with my colleagues ...

5 I think it would be a good job, interesting with lots of opportunity for travelling – but right now I have to study hard for the IELTS, to go to university, to get my degree ...

6 I've travelled to different cities with my job. I once went to Tokyo for a meeting. That was an amazing experience, so different from Sao Paolo. The people are ...

7 My favourite [subject] was physics at school, but I'm planning to study computer science in the future.

5 Organising your talk

A Points 2 and 4 are irrelevant.

B **The correct order is:** went to see my boyfriend in a swimming competition; I wanted to support him; lots of races; he won the breastroke

Extra information: he was feeling nervous; had seen (a swimming competition) on TV; he was very slow in the freestyle

C The speaker forgets to mention that Stephan won second place in the high jump.

Extra information: sports day every year; many students competed in different races; selected to take part by sports teacher; didn't win race because one of the teammates dropped the baton; winners given medals and prizes
Follow-up questions asked: Do you prefer to watch sport or take part? Are you good at football?

2 Education

LISTENING

1 Introduction

B **school:** report, project, uniform, pupil, classroom
university: seminar, tutor, lecture theatre
both: canteen, exams, term, coursework, assignment, timetable, library

2 Anticipating what you will hear

E 1 Sara; 2 Walker; 3 19 Swan Street; 4 18; 5 modern dance; 6 5th September

3 Following instructions carefully

1 No error; 2 A; 3 B; 4 No error; 5 C; 6 C

4 Identifying keywords and paraphrase

B 2 C

5 Form completion

1 Tufnell; 2 7th July 1987; 3 12, Castle Street; 4 OX4 2JP; 5 72388; 6 Grade B; 7 History

6 Multiple-choice questions with single answers

8 A; 9 B; 10 A

WRITING

1 Introduction

A undergraduate and postgraduate; B a first;
C balancing work and study; challenging job market; achieving a good degree

2 Understanding visual information

A Figure 1: Times Higher Education Supplement/Higher Education Statistics Agency

Figure 2: THES/Sodexho Lifestyle Survey 2004

B Blue shows the number of first class degrees achieved per year; red shows the number of upper-second degrees. The number refers to the total number of degrees awarded altogether.

C The vertical axis shows the number of students; the horizontal axis shows the year in which the results were recorded.

D The percentage of students who rated this problem as their number one worry.

E Total percentage is 88%. The remaining 12% of students might have cited a variety of other concerns that are statistically unimportant.

3 Writing the introduction

A **1** False; **2** True

C Suggested answer:

The bar chart presents the main concerns facing higher education students in 2004, ranging from pressure to succeed due to financial cost to worries about achieving their desired degree classification.

4 Organising the main body text

A **1 a** The correct order is: b, a, c.

2 a *This concern* refers to the students' biggest concern, i.e. worry about achieving the desired degree classification.

b *One* refers to students' biggest worry.

c *These figures* refer to 29%, 14% and 14%.

B **1** day-to-day financial worries; debt at graduation; pressure to succeed due to financial cost

2 26%

3 balancing academic, social and work commitments, day-to-day financial worries

C Suggested answer:

Not surprisingly, the question of money is a very big worry for students as it is mentioned in three separate categories (debt at graduation, day-to-day financial worries and pressure to succeed due to financial cost of university). Taken altogether, 26% of students rated these three categories as their number one concern. The joint third biggest concern for students is the day-to-day worries about money and the problem of balancing academic, work and social commitments, which 9% of students said was their biggest worry.

5 Comparing graphs

A **1** The pie charts compare the breakdown in the number of full-time and sandwich students with the number of part-time students who studied in higher education in the UK in the academic year 2002–03. Student numbers are broken down into three groups: first degree students, other undergraduates and postgraduates.

2 The key information is:

• There were many more full-time students than part-time (nearly double).

• The majority of full-time students were taking their first degree, whereas the minority of part-time students were taking their first degree.

• Other undergraduates were the minority of full-time students, for part-time students they were a much more significant group.

B **1** from an overall perspective; **2** in terms of the figures; **3** the former; **4** more specifically; **5** in comparison to

Suggested answer:

The majority of full-time and sandwich students were taking their first degree whereas for part-time students, it was the minority. As a mirror reflection, we can see that over 50% of part-timers were 'other undergraduates' while for full-timers, they represented roughly 10%. There was a similar picture for postgraduate part-time students who were more numerous both in absolute and relative terms than full-timers.

C **2 Suggested answer:** The bar chart shows the ten most popular education institutions in the UK for foreign students in the academic year 2002–03. The accompanying table shows the top ten education institutions that have recorded the highest growth in overseas student numbers in the same year.

3 Suggested answers:

• Nottingham had the highest number of overseas students whilst Wolverhampton had the highest increase in overseas students.

• Wolverhampton had by far the biggest increase in overseas students in the UK, more than twice the increase than second place Salford.

• Middlesex had the lowest number of overseas students compared to other institutions listed, although it had the tenth highest in the UK overall.

• Nottingham had about one third more overseas students compared to Middlesex.

6 Academic Writing Task 1: Report

A model answer is provided in the Writing Bank and in the Teacher's Guide.

3 Technology

READING

2 Locating information in the text

A **2** e; **3** c; **4** a; **5** b

B You would expect to find the answers in the following paragraphs: **a** 3/4; **b** 3; **c** 2/4; **d** 2/3; **e** 2/4

The answers are: **a** 4; **b** 5; **c** 1; **d** 2; **e** 3

C 1 Wi-fi; **2** (digital) camera; **3** music and video; **4** sharp clear screen; **5** docking station

D 1 because the product names appear too frequently throughout the passage

2 The keywords in the text are: **1** Internet connection; **2** good value for money; **3** broad product range/variety of models; **4** optional extra; **5** PC

The answers are: **1** C; **2** C; **3** A; **4** A; **5** B

3 Linking visual information to the text

B second half of Paragraph 3

C 1 clockwise; **2** Label 1 – adjective; Label 2 – noun

D 1 phosphor-coated; **2** cathode element; **3** beams

4 Labelling a diagram

1 front glass; **2** RGB filters; **3** liquid crystal cells; **4** white fluorescent light; **5** micro-transistors

5 Table completion

6 biggest; **7** 88%; **8** growth rate; **9** on the screen **10** prices; **11** screen(s)/screen size; **12** easily wall-mounted

6 Classification

13 B; **14** B; **15** B; **16** C; **17** A; **18** B

SPEAKING

2 Introducing the topic

A 2

B Let me see, I'd like to talk about ...; OK, I'm going to tell you about ...; Right, I'd like to tell you about ...; OK then, I want to talk about ...;

4 Expressing opinion

C In my view ...; I doubt ...; I believe ...; Personally, I think ...; I guess ...; I'm not sure if ...; In my opinion; For me ...

5 Comparing and contrasting information

A in some ways ... is also more ... than

B 1 quicker; cheaper than; more time-consuming than

2 are similar in that; not as enjoyable as; one of the main differences is that

3 However; whereas; much cheaper

4 on the other hand

4 The Workplace

LISTENING

2 Identifying signpost words

A 3 a first; **b** and; **c** next; **d** finally

B listing: first, finally; **adding:** and; **sequencing:** next

D 1 date; **2** contact details; **3** email

3 Following a description

A 1 left to right (clockwise); **2** 3

B 1 anti-slip; **2** pencil drawer; **3** five-star

4 Flowchart completion

1 group; **2** presentation; **3** mental processes; **4** interview; **5** offered the position; **6** References

5 Label completion

1 input; **2** rotating; **3** (heated) metal; **4** guiding pins; **5** take up

WRITING

3 Writing the opening paragraph

A 1 C; **2** A; **3** B

4 Presenting and justifying your opinion

A a 3; **b** 1; **c** 4; **d** 2

5 Expressing disagreement

A Suggested answers:

1 ... many employees do not work hard because their performance is not monitored.

2 ... there are others who would perform better if their work was rewarded financially according to results.

3 ... it doesn't mean that it is not beneficial to the education of children.

4 ... I would like to point out that people are still required to check that everything is working properly.

5 ... there are many people who work for little or no money at all.

6 ... targets and expectations of productivity have increased, so people are still putting in the same number of hours.

B Suggested answers:

a Although it may be true that people do not use

drama skills directly in their work lives, education is more than about preparing children for work.

b The argument that women should only be home-makers is an old-fashioned one and is a discriminatory remark against 50 per cent of the adult population.

6 Writing the conclusion

A Conclusion 1 rephrases the introduction and summarises the main points. Conclusion 2 contains new information and doesn't paraphrase the introduction.

7 Academic Writing Task 2: Essay

A model answer is provided in the Writing Bank and in the Teacher's Guide.

5 Climate and the Environment

READING

1 Introduction

B 2 **attitude:** b, c, e, f, j; **action:** a, d, g, h, i

2 Analysing meaning

B 1 Not given; 2 Yes; 3 No

C 1 Not given; 2 Yes; 3 Yes

3 Identifying paraphrase

C 1 e; 2 d; 3 b; 4 a; 5 c

4 Yes/No/Not Given

1 Yes; 2 No; 3 Yes; 4 Not given; 5 No; 6 No; 7 Not given

5 Sentence Completion

8 fuels; 9 causes of death; 10 impose a tax; 11 low-carbon technologies; 12 fuel-cell cars; 13 E; 14 F; 15 H; 16 A

SPEAKING

2 Describing and explaining

B 1 The reason why I don't like ... is ...
2 One of the things I love about this ... is ...

3 Speculating

A 1 speculate; 2 compare and contrast

B The first student's answer is better as it uses more language of speculation. (See examples in the language box in 3D.)

C probably not; it's very unlikely that; might; probably won't

4 Communicating your ideas clearly

B 1 *there are two main problems; firstly; in addition to this*

2 *for instance; such as*

3 *as a result; which will mean*

4 *this is due to*

6 Globalisation

LISTENING

2 Listening and writing simultaneously

A–C 1 Future Is Bright; 2 Dr Jack Jones; 3 Black Books; 4 1999; 5 2nd

3 Identifying distractors

B 1 smaller companies
D 2 weakens; 3 seed companies

4 Understanding meaning

A 1 T; 2 F; 3 F; 4 F; 5 F; 6 F

B 1 C; 2 A; 3 B; 4 A; 5 A

5 Classification

1 A; 2 B; 3 B; 4 B

6 Sentence completion and notes completion

5 (really) well researched; 6 support his argument; 7 academic; 8 bibliography; 9 Right or Wrong; 10 1,500; 11 February 2nd; 12 internal post

WRITING

2 Describing trends

A The line graph shows the change in the share price of Nokia in US dollars between March 2004 and March 2005.
1 price of each share in US dollars; 2 one year from March 2004 to March 2005; 3 past tenses (mostly past simple) because the period has finished; 4 most important: March 2004; August 2004, 5 March 2005 is lower than the previous year; 6 a decline in share price; 7 an increase in share price 8 March – April saw a peak, then a general fall with some levelling off until August; August onwards – a general increase until December; some fluctuations with downward movement until February; February to March recovered (back to December levels)

B Suggested answers:

1 a peak and then general fall with some levelling off until August

2 fell overall

3 There were some fluctuations but the price remained fairly constant/there was little change

4 There was a gradual increase/upward trend/rise

C 1 price of each share in US dollars; **2** one year from March 2004 to March 2005; **3** past tense; **4** There were a number of peaks in the share price during this period. However, the most significant trough was a fall in price to just $14 a share in mid-August. **5** March saw a lower share price than the same month of the previous year; **8** March to June saw a number of fluctuations, then a significant drop till August; prices rose until October when the price remained more stable until the end of the period.

D Suggested answers:

1 a decrease/downward trend/decline/fall; **2** several fluctuations; **3** sudden increase/rise; **4** general downward trend; **5** fell to the lowest point; **6** rise/increase; **7** reached a peak; **8** downward

3 Describing a process

A 1 Since 'Launch product …' is obviously the end, the process starts with 'Business plan'.

2 6; with sequence linking words (e.g. first, next)

3 present tenses – it is a general fact

4 Suggested answer: the steps a company should take to successfully launch a new product worldwide.

B Suggested answers:

1 in order to; **2** first; **3** Next; **4** Then/After that; **5** such as; **6** Once/When; **7** for example

The passive voice is used when the subject did not do the action. It is usually used to make something sound more formal and is common in processes.

4 Academic Writing Task 1: Report

A model answer is provided in the Writing Bank and in the Teacher's Guide.

7 Communication

READING

1 Introduction

B 1 by comparing skull sizes; **2** Not given

2 Identifying distracting information

A 1 Options a and b appear in the text but do not answer the question.

2 Option c appears in the text and answers the question.

B 1 Options a and b are not mentioned in the text.

2 Option c appears in the text and answers the question.

3 Identifying arguments

A 1 mentioned; **2** not mentioned; **3** mentioned; **4** not mentioned

B 1 agrees; **2** not mentioned; **3** disagrees; **4** agrees

4 Multiple-choice questions with multiple answers

Options C, D and E support the theory.

5 Multiple-choice questions with single answers

4 A; **5** A

6 True/False/Not Given

6 True; **7** False; **8** True; **9** Not given; **10** False; **11** Not given

SPEAKING

1 Introduction

1 7000; **2** Mandarin: more than 1 billion speakers; **3** 4000; **4** 86%; **5** 6 million

4 Hypothesising, speculating and evaluating

A Question 1 is asking you to evaluate.
Question 2 is asking you to speculate.
Question 3 is asking you to hypothesise.

B 1 on the one hand/but then again/on balance

2 if everyone spoke/would be easier

3 would be able

8 Growth and Development

LISTENING

2 Identifying features of speech

A 1 pace; **2** stress; **3** pause

B and C For the (majority) of animals,/and I include human beings in this category,/the most (dramatic) (physical changes) actually happen (before) the organism is born./Is this (really) the case? Well, think about it!/A mature (adult) human does not look (that) different to a (newborn baby),/but a newborn baby looks (nothing like) a fertilised (egg)!

3 Using features of speech

A For that is what we are at the time of our conception/– a (tiny, microscopic fertilised egg)/ Quite amazing, isn't it?/In the following (nine) (months) before our birth,/not only do we grow (hundreds of times) in size,/but we go through (three distinct) stages of development. The (first)/as I have just mentioned,/is the fertilised eggs./Then around a fortnight (after) conception,/the egg begins to repeatedly divide itself to become a mass of cells/known as the (embryo)/(Two) (months) later, this embryo has grown to approximately (2cm) long and is referred to as a (foetus.)

B 1 egg; **2** three; **3** mass of cells

D 4 8cm; **5** baby; **6** cry

E B; D; E; F (in any order)

4 Short-answer questions

1 brain; **2** muscles; **3** skeleton

5 Multiple-choice questions with multiple answers

4–7: C; D; E; F (in any order)

6 Summary completion

8 world; **9** the environment; **10** body parts

WRITING

2 Deciding the approach

A thesis-led: 1 and 3; argument-led: 1, 2, 3, 4

B 1 a is thesis-led; b is argument-led
  2 a matches Question 3; b matches Question 4
  3 Argument-led essay: Many people think, It is generally considered that
    Thesis-led essay: I believe, In my opinion, I totally disagree with

C Suggested answer:

Many people feel that the gap in understanding between the older and younger generation is too wide to be bridged. In the first case, the question assumes that there always is a 'gap' and that it needs to be 'bridged'. In the second case, we need to look more specifically at what is meant by 'older' and 'younger' people. Are we talking about differences between teenagers and middle-aged people, or differences between young adults and middle-age people?

3 Providing supporting evidence

A 1

B 1 A good example of this is; **2** for instance; **3** but this is not the case for; **4** From my experience; **5** highlights the point

C main idea: different generations have different experiences = generation gap

Supporting info: technology used differently by different generations; young people brought up with technology – older people were not; personal example of parents not knowing how to program a VCR and slow at texting.

D Suggested answer:

Another main reason why some people think the generation gap is unbridgeable is because both older people and younger people like it that way. Naturally many older people are in positions of authority as parents or bosses and think that if they keep a distance from their children or younger employees they will be respected by them. Younger people, in the same vein, aim to keep a distance from their parents or bosses because they don't want them to know all the details of their lives, as they fear they will be judged and punished if they do.

E 1 b, d; **2** a, c

4 Academic Writing Task 2: Essay

A model answer is provided in the Writing Bank and in the Teacher's Guide.

1 Leisure Activities

1.1

1 Candidate 1: Yeah, I just have one brother. He has two children, er ... sons, Juan and José, that makes me the uncle! I really like playing with his children, but it's always good to give them back to him at the end of the day! When I'm older I'd like to have some children myself, maybe two boys and a girl. I think that having children ...

2 Candidate 2: I really enjoy speaking it, and I like it when I learn a new word which is very useful or is funny in some way. But it's very hard work and sometimes I feel like I don't get better, er ... I'm not making a lot of progress. I prefer studying economics, which is the subject I'm hoping to study when I go to university next year. You know, it's interesting to learn about ...

3 Candidate 3: Not really, I'm not very sporty. I prefer to spend time playing on my computer. In fact, I really enjoy video games. I got a new game recently – it's really great. You're a criminal and you have to drive your car really fast about a city, and then sometimes escape from the police. It's very exciting. Sometimes I play with my friends, but it's quite difficult to ...

4 Candidate 4: I work in McDonald's. It's a part-time job. It's very good because it gives me time to study and I meet people to practise my speaking, you know, talking with my colleagues ...

5 Candidate 5: I don't know exactly what I want to do, but when I'm older I'd like to work for an international agency – I think it would be a good job, interesting with lots of opportunity for travelling – but right now I have to study hard for the IELTS, to go to university, to get my degree ...

6 Candidate 6: I'm from Sao Paolo in Brazil. I've travelled to different cities with my job. I once went to Tokyo for a meeting. That was an amazing experience, so different from Sao Paolo. The people are ...

7 Candidate 7: I really enjoy science subjects: chemistry, physics and biology. My favourite was physics at school, but I'm planning to study computer science in the future.

1.2

Candidate: OK, let's see. I want to tell you about the time I went to see my boyfriend take part in a swimming competition. It was part of a charity event – you know, making money for good causes. Anyway, why did I go? Well, I wanted to support him, to shout and cheer: it was his first big competition and he was feeling a little bit, er ... nervous. So, it was the first time I had been to such an event. I had seen it on the TV before of course, but when I saw it in real life it was very exciting indeed! I saw many different styles – crawl, this is freestyle, I think ... are they the same? And I saw breaststroke and backstroke and the butterfly. It was fantastic, you know? He was in the breaststroke competition and the freestyle. He was very slow in the freestyle, but the breaststroke competition, he won! It was very exciting and I felt very proud.

1.3

(C = Candidate; E = Examiner)

C: Er, let's see. I want to tell you about when I was at school. We had a sports day every year when many students competed in lots of different races and other things. Why did I go? Well, I used to be quite a fast runner in those days and so I had been selected to take part by a sports teacher of mine. I was chosen to run the 400-metre race where you have to give the baton to another person who is running – do you say 'relay race'? Unfortunately we didn't win as one of my teammates dropped the baton!

So, what did I see? Well, if you weren't taking part in the competition you sat on the grass in the sunshine and enjoyed the other races and events! I saw many of my friends do things like the long jump and high jump. At the end of the day all the winners were given medals and prizes. I really enjoyed it – it was fun because it was during the summer and I enjoyed not being in class and relaxing in the sunshine watching our mini Olympic games!

E: Do you prefer to watch sport or take part?

C: I like both, I think. I often play football with my friends and I like to watch it on TV, too.

E: Are you good at football?

C: I'm OK. I don't score many goals, but I enjoy it anyway.

2 Education

2.1

You will hear a student enrolling on a course.

2.2

2.2

(Sec = Secretary; St = Student)

Sec: Hello, come in.

St: Good morning. Are you the enrolment secretary?

Sec: I am.

St: I'm not too late to enrol on a course, am I?

Sec: No. We'll be enrolling new students till the end of the week.

St: Oh, thank goodness!

Sec: Have you done one of our courses before?

St: Oh no, this is my first time: the first step of my brilliant career.

Sec: Well, let's hope so. First though, we have to fill in a form.

St: Forms! They're so boring!

Sec: But necessary, I'm afraid.

2.3

(Sec = Secretary; St = Student)

Sec: Hello, come in.

St: Good morning. Are you the enrolment secretary?

Sec: I am.

ST: I'm not too late to enrol on a course, am I?

Sec: No. We'll be enrolling new students till the end of the week.

V2: Oh, thank goodness!

Sec: Have you done one of our courses before?

St: Oh no, this is my first time: the first step of my brilliant career.

Sec: Well, let's hope so. First though, we have to fill in a form.

St: Forms! They're so boring!

Sec: But necessary, I'm afraid. Now, what is your first name?

St: Sara, no 'h'.

Sec: Sorry?

St: S-a-r-a. Sara.

Sec: OK. Now your family name?

St: But I'm thinking about changing it to Simone, or maybe Sylvia.

Sec: Well, I think Sara's fine. So, what's your family name?

St: My family name is Walker.

Sec: W-a-l-k-e-r?

St: Yes.

Sec: OK. Now, where do you live?

St: Oh, yes, it's nineteen, one nine, Swan Street, London.

Sec: Swan?

St: Yes, like the bird.

Sec: OK, and your postcode?

St: N8 6BY.

Sec: N8 6BY ... And how old are you?

St: 18, well ... 19 next month.

Sec: So, 18. And what course would you like to do, Sara?

St: Well, I woke up this morning and said to myself, 'Now Sara, what are you going to do with your life? What course are you going to do?' My Dad thinks I should become a financial advisor and do people's accounts, because I'm pretty good with figures. Or perhaps I should be some kind of biologist, because that was my best subject at school. Or should I pursue my real love, modern dance?

Sec: And you chose modern dance.

St: Yes, I did. I want to make my living as a dancer.

Sec: Good for you. Now the course starts in the first week in September, which is ... let me see ... the fifth.

St: Oh, great. I can't wait.

Sec: Now, hold on! You have to be accepted onto the course first. You'll need to come in for an audition and interview.

St: Oh, no! I hate auditions.

Sec: I'm afraid if you want to be a dancer they're all part of the job!

St: Ah, well. When can they see me?

2.4

(Sec = Secretary; St = Student)

Sec: And what course would you like to do, Sara?

St: Well, I woke up this morning and said to myself, 'Now Sara, what are you going to do with your life? What course are you going to do?' My Dad thinks I should become a financial advisor and do people's accounts, because I'm pretty good with figures. Or perhaps I should be some kind of biologist, because that was my best subject at school. Or should I pursue my real love, modern dance?

Sec: And you chose modern dance.

St: Yes, I did. I want to make my living as a dancer.

Sec: Good for you.

2.5

(N = Nigel; R = Receptionist)

R: Hello! Hello, can I help you?

N: Yeah, I just wanted to ... is this where you apply for courses?

R: Well, it depends what course you want to take.

N: Um ..., business administration.

R: Fine. Take a seat and we'll complete all the necessary forms.

N: Oh, ... thanks!

R: Now, what's your first name?

N: Nigel.

R: Nigel. OK. And last name?

N: Tufnell.

R: Sorry ... ?

N: Tufnell. T-U-F-N-E-L-L

R: And when were you born?

N: When was I born? Er, 7th July 1987.

R: OK and you're male. And you were born in the UK?

N: Yeah. British.

R: And your first language is English?

N: Er ... yeah.

R: Address?

N: 12, Castle Street, Oxford.

R: Postcode?

N: Oh, no! I knew you were going to ask me that. I can never remember it! It's OX4 ... OX4 ... 2PG. No! OX4 ... 2JP. That's it!

R: Sure?

N: Positive.

R: Your phone number?

N: Oh, that's easy! 01865 72388 (double eight).

R: Now, qualifications. Any 'A' levels?

N: Yeah. Three.

R: Subjects and grades, please.

N: Um ... maths, B. Economics the same and then er, history ...

R: And what did you get for that?

N: E.

R: Oh, dear. Well, at least you passed.

N: Yeah.

2.6

(N = Nigel; R = Receptionist)

R: And it's business administration you want to do, isn't it?

N: Business administration. That's right, yes.

R: That's code, code ... let me just check ... yes, BA010. OK, the next course starts next semester. That's the fourth of October.

N: How long does it last?

R: A full academic year.

N: A year?

R: An *academic* year. That's around nine months.

N: Oh. OK. Good. Good.

R: Now all I need from you is a cheque covering the cost of the course, which is £2,500.

N: I didn't realise you'd need it today.

R: Well, you don't have to pay it all right now, but obviously you need to pay before you start the course and there are only a limited number of places, so ...

N: Can I give you a deposit?

R: A 10% deposit would secure your place, yes.

N: Is there a bank round here?

R: There's a cashpoint. Go out of this building. Turn left. Go past the library, and the cashpoint is just by the main lecture theatre, opposite the canteen.

N: OK. I'll ... I'll go and get the money.

R: You'd better hurry; the office is closing in five minutes.

N: OK, won't be long.

3 Technology

3.1

1 Candidate 1: Er, let me see: I'd like to talk about when I got an email from my father, you see I was travelling around the United States and I had asked him to send me some money ...

2 Candidate 2: <u>OK, I'm gonna tell you about an email I sent to my boss.</u> Basically, I was unhappy about some of the things he was asking me to do. I mean, I had spent all morning photocopying documents, which really wasn't my job …

3 Candidate 3: <u>Right, I'd like to tell you about the time I wrote an email to my landlord.</u> The problem was that I had moved out of his apartment one month before, but he still hadn't returned my deposit. I decided that I would tell him …

4 Candidate 4: <u>OK then, I want to talk about an email I got from an ex-boyfriend.</u> Where shall I begin? It was about two years after we had split up and I was living in a different city and everything. Anyway, I got this email which said how he still loved me and that he wanted to try again, so I …

3.2

1 Student 1: Yes, of course, it is now completely different – <u>personally, I think</u> email has made written communication much faster and cheaper than before. Firstly, you can write to someone on the other side of the world, and with one click, the information arrives seconds later, and secondly it costs you very little – just the connection to the Internet.

2 Student 2: Well, <u>I'm not sure if</u> this has improved the way students learn or not. <u>I guess</u> things are similar in that if students want to learn, they still have to go to class, read and make essays, etc, but I suppose on the other hand everything is now done on computer and is not written by hand. Learning is certainly more convenient though.

3 Student 3: It's a good question, but yes, <u>I think</u> it has. I can imagine a time very soon, when everyone will use videophones, it will be much more useful than only hearing a voice. If it is used a lot in business, you can have face-to-face meetings when you are very far apart. This will save a lot of time and money for travelling to meetings.

4 Student 4: <u>I doubt</u> that those people who can't use a computer will find office work easily. However, there will always be jobs where you don't need to use one, for example manual jobs where you use your hands to make things – like a construction worker or something like that.

5 Student 5: <u>I believe</u> things have changed dramatically. For example, it was only a few years ago that students would have to use books to find

information, whereas today, the Internet is the first place students go. This must be a good thing, so yes, <u>in my opinion</u>, things have improved.

6 Student 6: <u>In my view</u>, it's not as easy to find a job if you cannot use a computer because you do not have the skills most companies require. I mean, you cannot communicate well if you cannot use email … and another thing is perhaps you have to use a database.

7 Student 7: <u>For me</u> it's much easier to do research these days, you know, to find things. Before, it was more difficult to find things out. What I mean to say is, you had to read many journals to find the information you were searching for.

3.3

1 Candidate 1: I think email has changed the way we communicate at work. Of course it's much <u>quicker and cheaper than</u> writing a letter. When we get to work, there can be lots of emails to respond to, so I suppose in some ways email is also <u>more time-consuming than</u> before.

2 Candidate 2: Going to a library and using the Internet <u>are similar in that</u> they are both great sources of information. Maybe I'm old-fashioned, but I prefer reading a book to an article on a computer screen. The Internet is fantastic, but it's <u>not as enjoyable as</u> going to a library. I suppose <u>one of the main differences is that</u> you can hold a book, y'know, pick it up and turn the pages …

3 Candidate 3: Video mobiles are great fun, I use mine all the time. <u>However,</u> they are expensive. My bill last month was $100, <u>whereas</u> normal phone calls are <u>much cheaper.</u>

4 Candidate 4: Training people to be computer literate is expensive in the short term; <u>on the other hand</u>, it will eventually benefit the national economy.

4 The Workplace

4.1

Hello. On behalf of myself and my colleagues at the buildings administration department, I'd like to welcome you all to the new company headquarters. Now, here in this brand new complex, we have a wealth of flexible facilities and space available for use. So, if you need a small meeting room for two people or a presentation suite for up to fifty, we at buildings admin. can help. However, we would ask that you don't just go into an empty room and start using it. We ask everybody to follow this simple room-booking procedure using the company intranet.

First, choose the sort of room you require and, most importantly, don't forget to tell us the time and ████ you'll be needing it. And you might also like to let us know if you have any special requirements – conference calling facilities, for example. Coffee and other refreshments are always available. But if you need sandwiches, a buffet or a sit-down lunch, you need to contact the catering department. Next, fill in the booking form with your ████████. This is an internal billing requirement, so please don't forget. Finally, you'll get confirmation of your room booking via ████. And that's it! Simple!

4.2

Hello. On behalf of myself and my colleagues at the buildings administration department, I'd like to welcome you all to the new company headquarters. Now, here in this brand new complex, we have a wealth of flexible facilities and space available for use. So, if you need a small meeting room for two people or a presentation suite for up to fifty, we at buildings admin. can help. However, we would ask that you don't just go into an empty room and start using it. We ask everybody to follow this simple room-booking procedure using the company intranet.

First, choose the sort of room you require and, most importantly, don't forget to tell us the time and date you'll be needing it. And you might also like to let us know if you have any special requirements – conference calling facilities, for example. Coffee and other refreshments are always available. But if you need sandwiches, a buffet or a sit-down lunch, you need to contact the catering department. Next, fill in the booking form with your contact details. This is an internal billing requirement, so please don't forget. Finally, you'll get confirmation of your room booking via email. And that's it! Simple!

4.3

Good morning, Ladies and Gentleman. Thanks for letting me come and talk to you today. My name's Bill Loman and, as most of you know, I represent Acme Office Supplies. It's our job to bring you the very best in office supplies and we do everything we can to make your working day just that little bit more pleasant.

Now, do you have to move around from one part of the building to another? Do you ever wish you could take

your desk with you, along with your laptop and other essential bits and pieces? Would be great, wouldn't it? Well, now you can, with this – the Mobile Office! It's ideal for any situation where the user sits, stands or moves about.

Take a closer look at it. This is a ruggedly constructed, highly adaptable unit. At the top is a flat work surface, where you can put your laptop computer and still have plenty of room for some files or documents. And you don't need to worry about your laptop accidentally getting knocked off because the laptop area is covered with a heavy-duty anti-slip rubber. There's even an optional laptop cable lock available. What's more, you can easily rotate the surface to cater for left and right-handed users. Now, chances are you may have to carry around all sorts of other bits and pieces – pens, erasers, a stapler, a hole punch, etc. Well, the Mobile Office can help you out there, too, with a storage option under the work surface. There are a range of options available, depending on the model, but they include a single utility drawer, a double utility drawer or, as shown here, a pencil drawer.

Now, some of us are short, some of us are tall. Sometimes we need to stand, others prefer to sit. So the desktop work surface is mounted on a fully adjustable stand. This means you can vary the height of the surface between 30 and 42 inches. The stand is mounted on top of a five-star castor base, making the whole unit fully mobile. And if you are worried about the unit moving during use you can also opt for locking castors, keeping the whole thing as solid as a rock.

The next thing I'd like you to see is this. Now, if you've got a lot of confidential documents, you can't just throw them away ...

4.4

Part of my job as Human Resources Coordinator at the local Bob's Brushes factory is to recruit or select new members of staff. Today, I'd like to explain how our selection process works.

In the old days, if you went along for a job, you normally just got an interview. They asked you a few questions and that was it. But an interview does not give a true indication of a candidate's behaviour. For example, a candidate may say they are very good at doing presentations. But are they really? You need to see them in action. So, we like to put our candidates through what's called a recruitment process. This usually takes a whole day and consists of a number of stages.

First of all, candidates are normally presented with a

group exercise, because it's important to see if they can work well in a team. Then they are asked to deliver a brief presentation. Candidates are given advance notice of this so that they can prepare.

Next is a role-play. In this exercise, candidates are put into a difficult situation they might find themselves in if they are appointed to the position. Following this, candidates are set a series of psychometric tests, which assess their mental processes to see if they have the right skills for the job.

After all this, candidates attend an interview alone with a panel of three to four members of personnel from different departments. At the end of the day, candidates are thanked and sent home with a bag of Bob's Brushes goodies.

Then comes the tricky part – we have to choose someone for the position. We analyse all the data and information we now have for each candidate. Sometimes none of the candidates are right for the job and we have to go through the whole process again. However, usually we find the right person and the successful applicant is offered the position. Unsuccessful candidates are also sent feedback on their performance. They may not have been successful this time, but we may need them in the future.

The final stage is taking up references. Unless we discover from a referee that a candidate has lied on their CV, or has some kind of shady past, the candidate takes up their new position in a month or so. Job done. The post is filled. Now, any questions?

4.5

Well, the next stop on our tour of Bob's Brushes is the production department and I thought I'd just show you this. Each and every brush which leaves the factory has our logo on the handle. In the old days, applying them used to be a manual task but these days it's all fully automated. It's called a 'logo machine' and at the moment it's set up for fixing logos onto the handles of 1½-inch paint brushes.

Let me tell you how it works. The paintbrush handles are placed into a large metal container just to the left of the conveyor belt there, called the 'input hopper'. This hopper vibrates, causing the handles to drop down a kind of funnel one by one onto a conveyor belt. This belt then carries the handles up into the main body of the machine. As they enter the machine, the handles move onto a rotating scroll. This rotating action realigns the handles and they are then carried along to the far end. At this point they are transferred to the handle wheel. This wheel carries the handles up in an anti-clockwise direction towards a metal roller,

which is heated, and this is where the logo is applied. Now, about these logos. The logos arrive from the suppliers on a long strip of special paper wound round a big drum. It works a bit like putting film into a camera. You see just to the right of the control station there? That's the 'logo strip payoff drum'. There're about 25,000 logos on that. From this, the logo strip is then fed round a series of what we call 'dancers', but what are technically referred to as 'guiding pins'. These are a very important part of the machine as it's crucial to maintain exactly the right tension in the logo strip. Anyway, the logo strip moves back towards the handle wheel and as it passes between the wheel and the roller, the logo is transferred to the handle. The waste strip, now empty of logos, carries on and is wound round the 'logo strip take up drum' on the far right there. And the brush handles? Well, after the logo is applied by the roller, they continue round and are unloaded through a special cylinder at the top left-hand side of the wheel, which blows them down a pipe into a waiting box at the back of the machine. Clever stuff: fast, simple, efficient.

OK, now have you ever wondered about how tooth brushes are made? Well, in the old days ...

5 Climate and the Environment

5.1

1 **Candidate 1:** The reason why I don't like this type of weather is that it saps all your energy, you know, you just feel like lying around the house all day, you feel really listless and you just don't get anything done. Either that, or you freeze to death! You see, if I'm at my parents' house, they always have the air conditioning turned up really high and it's just so cold. The other thing is we have this type of hot, humid weather all year round – the only difference is between the dry and the rainy season, but it's always hot and very sticky – really not very nice at all.

2 **Candidate 2:** One of the things I love about this hot sunny weather is feeling the sun on my face, you see in my country the winters are long and very, very cold, so it's always a relief to have some sunshine. I like going walking in the country with my husband. We both love nature and really enjoy the countryside when it's green and beautiful. The sunshine gives me energy and makes me feel happy. It's rarely too hot in my part of the country, so we just enjoy it as we know it's not going to last too long!

5.2

1 Candidate 1: The reason why I don't like this type of weather is that it saps all your energy, you know ...

2 Candidate 2: One of the things I love about this hot sunny weather is feeling the sun on my face, you see ...

5.3

1 Candidate 1: Er, probably not! Some governments have already made some changes, but in my view it's very unlikely that they will ever do enough. The problem is that, while governments might introduce green policies to win them more votes, for instance recycling waste, they probably won't commit themselves to policies that are unpopular with the voters. For instance, getting people out of their cars and onto buses and trains is always a very unpopular measure.

2 Candidate 2: I think it's very important that governments do something about climate change. The earth is getting warmer. The sea levels are rising and the weather is becoming much more violent and unpredictable. We need to do something about this problem before it's too late. There has been a lot of talk about this at international conferences, but nothing very much has been done.

5.4

1 Candidate 1: Er, probably not! Some governments have already made some changes, but in my view it's very unlikely that they will ever do enough. The problem is that, while governments might introduce green policies to win them more votes, for instance, recycling waste, they probably won't commit themselves to policies that are unpopular with the voters. For instance, getting people out of their cars and onto buses and trains is always a very unpopular measure.

5.5

1 Candidate 1: There are two main problems for the farmers: firstly, I think heavy rain causes the soil to be washed away, I mean the soil with all the minerals in it. In addition to this many plants rot in the ground because they never have time to dry. Think when it rains very heavily, for example in my country, it is very difficult for the farmers.

2 Candidate 2: There are things we can do to help slow global warming. For instance, we can stop using up all the coal and gas, and use cleaner energy such as power from the wind or sun.

3 Candidate 3: Rising temperatures will lengthen the food-growing season in some countries. As a result, farmers will be able to produce more crops which will mean less hunger in the world. I'm sure you'd agree this is a good thing ... er, a benefit.

4 Candidate 4: It's generally agreed that the earth is getting warmer, this is due to more and more greenhouse gases in the atmosphere.

6 Globalisation

6.1

(T =, Tutor; B = Brad; C = Janet)

T: OK. Before we all rush off on our holidays, I need to give you your reading assignment for the break.

B: Oh, no ... reading.

T: I'm afraid so, Bradley. Now, as you may be aware, there have been literally thousands of books published on the subject of globalisation. Some of the authors have become quite famous; Naomi Klein, for example, with her book 'No Logo', which became an international bestseller.

J: Oh, I've heard of that, I think my brother's got a copy. Maybe I could borrow it.

T: Yes, well why not? It's a fairly easy read. Another author, the Peruvian economist, Hernando de Soto, has some very interesting ideas on ways of eradicating poverty in third world countries by freeing up the assets tied up in buildings on land without any clear ownership. He's very influential and has worked closely with the likes of Bill Clinton in the past.

B: So, do you want us to read his book?

T: Not just yet, no. The first book I'd like you to read is called, 'The Future Is Bright, the Future Is Global'.

6.2

Tutor: They used to have a copy in the library, but I think it's disappeared. It's written by Dr Jack Jones, who used to lecture at this university.

6.3

Tutor: It was first published by Black Books, who are specialists in this kind of thing, in 1999. But please make sure you buy the second edition. The world changes so quickly these days. Now the other book is against globalisation. It's called, 'Hands off the Planet' by Ted Crilly.

It's published by Craggy Press and ...

6.4

(A = Alison; D = Dave)

D: Hi there, Alison?

A: Hello, Dave. Long time, no see. What've you been up to?

D: Oh, this and that. Research mainly.

A: Researching what?

D: The WTO.

A: World Trade Organisation?

D: Yes. It's all part of this project I'm doing on globalisation.

A: Oh, yeah. We did that last year. What do you make of it then?

D: Well, it's not exactly the most caring of organisations, is it?

A: What do you mean, Dave?

D: WTO rules favour the larger companies from wealthy countries.

A: In what way?

D: Well, by prohibiting protection through discriminatory tariffs, it's hard for poor countries to build up domestic industries.

A: That may be the case. But I'm sure that's not a deliberate policy. Anyway you could argue that the rules laid down by the World Trade Organisation don't exactly help smaller companies from the richer nations either.

D: Why not?

A: Well, many companies in wealthy countries, especially textile and clothing producers, oppose globalisation because they can't compete with cheaper imports made in countries with lower production costs.

D: ... like China.

A: Exactly.

6.5

(A = Alison; D = Dave)

D: Ah. And that's another thing!

A: What is?

D: Democracy. The WTO isn't the most democratic of organisations, is it?

A: Why do you say that? You know, all of the WTO's rules have to be ratified by member states and all decisions are reached through consensus.

D: Yes, but all those decisions are made behind closed doors.

A: Maybe, Dave. But I still believe that the WTO is a force for strengthening democracy throughout the world, as it encourages international trade and therefore the exchange of ideas and beliefs, including democracy.

D: I can't see how you arrive at that conclusion, Alison. No, if you ask me, it's quite the opposite. The WTO actually weakens the democratic process because it allows the formation of enormous multinational organisations that are richer and more powerful than some countries. And that can't be good. When it comes to global democracy, the WTO has a weakening effect.

A: I suppose you're going to tell me that the WTO should regulate international companies over pollution next.

D: And so they should. The WTO allows global companies to locate pollution-producing industries in poor countries.

A: This idea is nonsense, Dave. Why would a company choose to relocate a whole plant to the other side of the world. The cost would be enormous. It would be much cheaper for the company to clean up the existing plant.

D: Maybe, but look at the extensive logging of the rainforests, Alison. You must agree that the WTO should regulate that?

A: The WTO's regulations allow for countries to protect such natural resources. What does worry me is the way agricultural seed companies focus on high-yield, disease-resistant plants at the expense of other plants. This policy is destroying plant biodiversity and that can only spell trouble. No, these seed companies need regulating.

D: Well, at least we're agreed on something. Fancy a cup of coffee?

A: Only if it's Fairtrade.

D: What? In this place? You'll be lucky. Come on ...

6.6

1 **A:** Are the British happy with the conditions as laid out in the contract?

   B: Well, they said the terms were 'not unacceptable'...

2 **A:** And do you actually believe that the French would agree to such a deal?

   B: Well, it's not unheard of.

3 While the offer on the table is far from perfect, at the end of the day it's almost certainly the best we are going to get.

4 **A:** Mr Yamamoto, these designs are just what we need.

   B: I couldn't agree with you more, Señor Ramirez!

5 **A:** Mr Edwards, the Chinese have withdrawn their offer.

   B: Oh, great!

6 **A:** Mr Edwards, the Japanese have withdrawn their offer.

   B: Oh, great!

6.7

(K = Katya; P = Peter)

K: OK, Peter, we need to decide about our presentation next week.

P: OK, Katya. What do you think we should talk about?

K: Well, Dr Chobham said to look at some of the factors that have contributed to the process of globalisation.

P: Er, yes. I was thinking maybe we could do something on the Internet.

K: Really?

P: Yeah, along with things like satellite TV and cheap flights, I'd say the Internet was really important in terms of globalisation.

K: I think you've got something there, Peter. I mean anyone can get hold of all that information, anywhere on the planet.

P: All you need is a computer, a modem and a phone line.

K: Precisely.

6.8

(K = Katya; P = Peter)

K: And apparently, I was reading, the Internet and mobile telephones allow developing countries to leapfrog steps in the development of their infrastructure.

P: What does that mean?

K: Well, for example, the Philippines has a poor landline telephone system, but with a mobile phone and computer, you don't need to use it.

P: ... I don't even know anyone here who uses a computer with their mobile!

K: But in my book, the Internet has moved too far from its non-commercial roots. When it was created it was meant to be a tool for people to communicate with each other. These days it's dominated by big business which is only interested in selling you yet more stuff. I get so much junk mail, and all those pop-ups!

P: Oh, that doesn't bother me. I rather like to know what's on offer.

K: The Internet could also be seen as divisive.

P: In what way?

K: Well-off countries have much greater access to the Internet and communication services in general. What we are witnessing is an information revolution and less well-off countries are getting left behind.

P: Up to a point. Yes, not everyone has access to the Internet at home. But many places have shared communal access – some villages in Africa, for example. But on the whole, it's such a great way of exchanging ideas.

K: Ha! I think you'll find it's a one-way street. The vast majority of websites are in English and western values dominate.

P: I know, I know. You think it's a kind of cultural imperialism.

K: I think that's a fair assessment, don't you?

P: I think you're exaggerating the situation there, Katya. For me, and millions of other people, it's just an easy way of keeping in touch with family and friends, even when you are thousands of miles away.

K: Ah, that reminds me. It's my mum's birthday today. I forgot to send her a card!

P: Why not send her an electronic card?

K: Great idea! Where would we be without the Internet?

6.9

(T =, Tutor; B = Brad; J = Janet)

T: Welcome back. I trust you had a good break and that you managed to read the books I recommended to you. Any problems, Brad?

B: You know, I thought 'Hands off the Planet' might be difficult to get hold of. As it turned out, they had a whole stack of them in my local bookstore. It was even on special offer!

J: Yeah, and you get a free password to enter a website dedicated to the book.

T: Really, Janet?

J: Yeah, I tried to take a look at it but the link wasn't working.

T: Ah well, and what about Dr Jones' book?

B: The bookstore said it was reprinting at the moment. But in the end I managed to track down a copy in a second-hand bookshop.

T: Smart thinking there, Brad. How about you, Janet?

J: Well, my brother had a copy so I just borrowed that.

T: Good, so what did you make of them?

B: I loved 'Hands off the Planet', it was such an easy read, unlike 'The Future Is Bright'. I mean, it kept losing me, the argument just kept jumping around.

J: I know what you mean, it wasn't helped by the fact that quite a few of the quotes in foreign languages were left untranslated, it's as if we're all expected to be multilingual!

T: Yes I'm afraid that Dr Jones does like to show off his familiarity with different languages. I'll certainly make that point to him next time I see him.

J: But I think the main problem with Dr Jones' book was that it assumed a previous knowledge of the subject.

B: Yeah, right. There were some chapters where I felt way out of my depth. I had no idea what he was talking about.

J: I had to get my brother to explain it to me!

B: I just didn't feel Dr Jones' book was very user-friendly. Unlike 'Hands off the Planet', it had no illustrations and the section containing the extended interviews with all those foreign businessmen just went on and on.

J: Didn't it just!

T: Well, it is a little on the long side, yes, but I think it remains a relevant and valuable resource, though on reflection it may have been a wiser option to have put these in the back of the book.

J: As an appendix?

T: Precisely.

6.10

(T = Tutor; B = Brad; C = Janet)

T: So you preferred 'Hands off the Planet', did you, Brad?

B: Yeah, I thought it was really interesting. Crilly obviously spent an awful lot of time preparing this book, all those amazing facts and figures. The chapter on how cinema, TV and newspapers are becoming more global was really well researched. In fact I was shocked to read just how powerful and influential some of these media corporations are.

J: Yes, though I thought at times the author just conveniently overlooked any data that didn't support his argument. It seemed to be quite biased, I thought.

B: That's because he's passionate about all this. He's very concerned about the future of the planet.

J: Well, that's highly commendable, I'm sure. But oversimplifying things to such an extent greatly distorts the true picture, and by adopting so radical a position he can actually put people off.

B: Yes, but he sees it as his mission to make people sit up and take notice.

J: Well, to be honest, I'm surprised we were asked to read this book at all.

T: Really, Janet? What makes you say that?

J: It's quite lightweight, isn't it? I'm not surprised they had so many in the bookshop. I don't know, I just didn't find the tone academic enough for a serious study.

B: You mean you didn't like the Captain Planet comic strips? I thought they were hilarious!

J: Yes, I liked them. They were quite amusing. But I didn't think that they were particularly appropriate for a serious subject such as globalisation.

T: Hmm, I tend to agree with you there, Janet, but other students have read it in the past and most of them have been favourable towards it.

J: Another factor which I felt detracted from the academic nature of the book was that there was no index, whereas the one in Dr Jones' book is excellent.

B: Ah yes, it was superb. More than could be said for the bibliography in 'Hands off the Planet'. It's virtually non-existent.

T: Well maybe there's some more information on the website, if you can make it work that is. OK, thank you for your comments. All very interesting and most useful. Now if we could just focus in on some of the ideas expressed in these books ...

6.11

(T = Tutor; B = Brad; C = Janet)

B: ... especially with bananas and so on.

J: Oh, I know exactly what you mean.

T: OK. Time for us to wrap up. Now, I'd like you to write an essay. <u>The title is ... 'Globalisation: right or wrong?'.</u>

B: How many words?

T: <u>One thousand, five hundred.</u>

J: When is it for?

T: Where are we? January 21st. Shall we say in one week's time? The 28th?

B: Oh. I'm not sure, we've got exams till the 26th.

T: Fine. <u>Let's call it February 2nd.</u> That will give you the weekend.

J: OK. And do you want us to email it to you?

T: Best not to. We've had a few problems with the system in the past. No, pop it in the <u>internal post.</u> Right, I'd better hurry. I've got a lecture in five minutes, now where did I put my gloves?

7 Communication

7.1

1 Candidate 1: I think, <u>on the one hand,</u> we can do business more efficiently, but <u>then again,</u> other languages may die out, so <u>on balance I think</u> we need to monitor the situation more closely and make sure other languages survive.

2 Candidate 2: I suppose <u>if everyone spoke</u> the same language, it <u>would be easier</u> to do international business, I mean you wouldn't have to worry about having negotiations in a second language.

3 Candidate 3: In my opinion, political leaders <u>would be able</u> to relate to each other better. You know, sometimes it can be difficult to really connect with someone if you have to speak through an interpreter.

8 Growth and Development

8.1

For the majority of animals, and I include human beings in this category, the most dramatic physical changes actually happen before the organism is born. Is this really the case? Well, think about it! A mature adult human does not look that different to a newborn baby, but a newborn baby looks nothing like a fertilised egg!

8.2

For that is what we are at the time of our conception – a tiny, microscopic fertilized <u>egg</u>. Quite amazing, isn't it? In the following nine months before our birth not only do we grow hundreds of times in size, but we go through <u>three</u> distinct stages of development. The first as I have just mentioned, is the fertilized egg. Then around a fortnight after conception the egg begins to repeatedly divide itself to become a <u>mass of cells</u> known as the embryo. Two months later, this embryo has grown to approximately 2cm long and is referred to as a foetus.

8.3

Around the end of the first trimester, the foetus has grown to approximately <u>eight centimetres</u> in length and is beginning to resemble a miniature <u>baby</u>, complete with upper and lower limbs. After a further four months, in case you've lost track of where we are, that's seven months after conception, the foetus is approximately 40cm in length. What's more, by now it has a fully developed reflex system, giving the foetus the capacity to breathe, swallow and even <u>cry</u>. This is the reason why, if the mother gives birth prematurely – before the baby's full nine months is up – there is a good chance that it will survive and go on to lead a normal, healthy life, though it might need to live in an incubator for a few weeks.

8.4

When a baby is born, it can do only a fraction of what it can do in later life. Unlike other species – horses for example, which can walk within a few hours of being born – human babies take several months to learn how to crawl and several more before they can walk. Though fairly helpless, a newborn baby can see. And while its vision is not that developed when first born, it can usually make out faces up to 30cm away. A baby's ability to identify people is not just restricted to sight. Smell plays a part too and <u>newborn babies can identify particular smells</u> – its mother, for instance, and will <u>smile on her approach</u>. Many babies suck their thumbs. In fact, scans have revealed that some do this before birth. <u>They can also swim.</u> While this skill is quickly lost and has to be relearned in later life, when placed in water, babies will do a sort of doggie paddle, swimming a bit like a dog. Although newborns have a walking reflex – pregnant mothers often report feeling the baby 'kick' – what they can't do is walk, or even crawl or turn over. Movement of the head is restricted, too. The lifting of the head from a prone position cannot normally be achieved until around one month, though turning the head is within the range of most newborns.

8.5

Early pioneers described the development of an infant's motor skills in great detail. In the 1930s and 40s, Arnold Gesell identified 22 stages in the development of crawling, beginning with the lifting of the head from a prone position and ending with an even, balanced crawl on hands and feet. Myrtle McGraw, similarly identified seven primary stages in the development of walking, from a newborn's stepping movements to the baby's ability to walk independently by the end of its first year. For these pioneers, motor development was a consequence of neuromuscular maturation, that is mainly independent changes in an infant's brain, its muscles and last but not least its growing skeleton.

8.6

This theory of neuromuscular maturation became the popularly accepted explanation for motor development for the next forty years or so. It was not until the 1980s that new research methods and technologies allowed researchers to analyse and measure the development of infants' motor skills in a different way. One such way is the Dynamic Systems Approach, which was developed by the psychologist, Esther Thelen, building on the work of a Russian physiologist, Nicholai Bernstein. In this account, new motor skills are believed to emerge from the coming together of a variety of interacting factors. For example, in order for a child to walk independently a number of these factors must be in place: the child's muscles must be powerful enough to counteract the effects of gravity. As mentioned earlier, the stepping instinct is common in newborn babies, but they lack the bodily strength to maintain an upright position. However, when they are placed in water, thus making them lighter, they begin to make stepping motions. When they are removed from the water, the action ceases. The stepping reflex normally disappears after a few months. By the way, as I'm sure many of you will know, newborn babies can swim, however this ability is lost with age and has to be relearned. In order to walk a child should also have lost the top-heavy body proportions typical of infants. The resulting lowering of its centre of gravity gives it better balance and means that it does not have to hold on to things in order to remain upright. They also need a reason to walk. If the baby has no need to go anywhere, why

should it? Very young babies cannot see that well, but as its vision and brain matures, it can identify objects from a distance and so its interest is aroused. At the same time this improvement in perception makes it more aware of its environment. In other words it can identify the nature of its surroundings and the type of terrain it needs to traverse, making progress possible.

8.7

Perception plays a more important role in another approach to motor skills development – the Perception-Action approach, which was inspired by the work of Jane and Eleanor Gibson. For them, there is a strong correlation between our perception of the world around us and our ability to perform movement within it. In other words, our ability to move is not just down to the physical development of our bodies, but also our perceptual ability. For an action to be planned and executed successfully, we need to have perceptual information about certain properties of the environment, our bodies and the relationship between the two. At the same time, we usually acquire sensory information through the use of movement. For example, we may use exploratory movement of body parts such as the hands, feet, eyes and head, to generate perceptual information in light, sound, muscles and skin. In a similar way, actions generate more information for perceptual systems. Furthermore, motor development does not stop after infancy. After mastering basic postural, manipulative and locomotor skills, children acquire many more abilities: writing, playing an instrument, etc. While movement is stiff, wasteful and uncoordinated at first, with practice it becomes progressively more rhythmical, smooth and efficient.